# THE COMPLETE BOOK OF
# SHARK
# FISHING

Hammerhead sharks grow to awesome size and challenge an angler's skills to the utmost. Moments after this photo, the shark was released unharmed.

# THE COMPLETE BOOK OF
# SHARK
# FISHING

## MILT ROSKO

**Burford Books**

Printed in Canada

10  9  8  7  6  5  4  3  2  1

Library of Congress Cataloging-in-Publication Data

Rosko,  Milt.
 The complete book of shark fishing / Milt Rosko.
   p. cm.

  ISBN 1-58080-107-2 (hardcover)
  1.  Shark fishing.  I. Title.

SH691.S4 R67 2003
799.1'73--dc21

# Contents

# IN MEMORIAM

Captain Billy Verbanas was just 40 years old, happily married to Cindy, with six wonderful children when tragedy struck on July 9, 2002. He lost his life through drowning as a result of a mako shark dragging him into the sea as he took a wrap in attempt to pull it within range for gaffing.

Bill was a deeply religious person, who with his family worshiped at the Resurrection Parish in Newark, Delaware. He was always ready to help others. Persons in need and fellow fishermen all benefited from his willingness to share.

His many friends and associates felt it appropriate to establish a special trust fund to ensure that his children receive the education that he would have provided had not this tragedy occurred. Contributions to the fund may be made to The Fund for Capt. Billy's Kids, Wilmington Trust, 2371 Limestone Road, Wilmington, Delaware 19808. Additional information may be obtained by calling Sean Malone, 302-454-8661.

Capt. Billy Verbanas' children, left to right, include Jessica 10, Niki 8, Baby Joey 9 months, Sarah 9, Rachel 3, and Jacob 6.

_This book is respectfully dedicated
to the thousands of recreational anglers who enjoy
fishing for sharks and recognize the importance
of both preserving and conserving this valuable
resource for future generations._

# ACKNOWLEDGMENTS

It's really very difficult to acknowledge all of the people who played a role and in some way made a contribution to the knowledge I absorbed in order to compile this text.

There is one person in particular who has helped not only me, but also the thousands of anglers along the coast with whom he made contact in a very meaningful way when it came to shark fishing. As I began this treatise, I went through my files of shark correspondence and came across a letter yellowed with age and dated August 28, 1962. It was from John Casey, then a marine biologist headquartered at the Sandy Hook Marine Laboratory. I visited the lab often, located in the old buildings that once comprised Fort Hancock and protected the approaches to New York Harbor.

As a result of my having provided data on shark catches during that era, Jack had sent me a draft copy of *A Sportsman's Guide to Sharks,* which he and two associates had prepared. The guide was ultimately published and to this day is available from the National Marine Fisheries Service's marine laboratory at Narragansett, Rhode Island (see page 186).

Only if you know Jack could you come to appreciate his commitment to sharks and shark fishing. His attention to detail was infinite, whether he was examining the stomach contents of a shark just brought to dockside or the line art illustrating the minute differences between the mako and porbeagle shark. Importantly, he graciously shared his expertise with everyone, and I for one gratefully acknowledge the wealth of information he passed along.

Another person who warrants acknowledgment and who was perhaps the greatest shark hunter of them all was the late Frank Mundus. Frank would rather have fished for sharks from his *Cricket*—which he sailed from Shinnecock on Long Island, New York—than do anything else. He did more to popularize sportfishing for sharks on all three coasts than any other angler I've known. I'd be remiss were I not to say I expanded my knowledge of sharks and shark fishing as a result of his pioneering skills, which he graciously shared with everyone.

Frank collaborated with the late Bill Wisner, another dear friend, when they wrote *Sportfishing for Sharks*. The vintage tome can still be obtained from specialty firms that handle out-of-print titles, and it's a good read by two fine shark fishermen.

I'd also like to thank Alan Sherman for the fine artwork that appears throughout this book. Alan prepared the original art for my *Complete Book of Saltwater Fishing,* and because of his attention to detail we worked together again. I'm certain his drawings will help tie in much of the detail that is covered in the text.

Jennifer Basilio, my granddaughter, is a graphic arts major at Monmouth University. She's prepared the illustrations for several of my books, and is responsible for the excellent shark illustrations that appear in this book. Jenny's equally at home at her drawing table or along the surf, where she's beached many a dogfish while seeking more formidable game. My thanks to her for not only her interest but also the attention to detail she provides in her fine work.

My wife, June, also deserves my thanks, for much of the photography in this book is the result of her fine camera handling. We spent many a day, and night aboard our *Linda June* probing nearshore and offshore waters in quest of many finned adversaries. As this book goes to press, we will be approaching the 50th anniversary of the publication of my first magazine article, and happily our 50th wedding anniversary!

A special thank-you to the many shark anglers who shared their photos, tips, and experiences for inclusion herewith. Each of them shares with me the rewards of the contemplative pastime of shark fishing, which is what this book is all about.

# INTRODUCTION

If you've picked up this book, in all likelihood you're either a veteran shark fisherman or a newcomer anxious to get in on the ground floor of the exciting pastime of seeking the hundreds of species of sharks that are found in all the waters of the world. As the table of contents for this tome was being developed, I made a decision not to make it a dry, scientific journal. I wanted it to be a readable treatise that would enable both the veteran angler and the newcomer to absorb a wealth of information about the exciting sport of shark fishing. I also wanted to share many of my personal experiences and the challenges that were all a part of seeking these fine game fish. As I wrote the conclusion and began to review the text, I kept copying and pasting on the computer, adding a tip that was forgotten on the first pass and including many reminiscences that hopefully you'll find of interest.

You'll be the final judge as you peruse the pages. First is a natural history of sharks; after this came the hard part. Which sharks to include that were noteworthy of a sportfisherman's efforts? I've included 15 major species, but sprinkled throughout the text are many species that don't share their notoriety. Still, all of them have given me many memorable moments while on the water.

Chapters on selecting basic shark tackle, equipment, and boats are by no means exciting, but they're extremely important, as successful shark fishermen hone their skills bringing all three components into play. Today's shark anglers are fortunate in that they can benefit from the age of electronics and modern technology to aid in their quest, something I wasn't able to do more than half a century ago.

Once you position yourself in an area frequented by sharks, whether from a boat or shore, it all comes down to using a wide variety of techniques to attract these residents of the seven seas to your bait or lure. I believe I've included a series of strategies and techniques that will enable you to really enjoy this sport to the maximum. After absorbing everything between the covers, it all comes down to getting out on the water, putting in the time, applying the techniques, and enjoying the sport.

As you get to know shark fishermen, I believe you'll join me in the realization that they are a rugged fraternity of angler. Indeed, shark fishermen are a breed unlike any other in the sportfishing community. I've been fortunate to have known many fine shark fishermen and fished with them in variety of picturesque, exotic locales. It's been fun, and that's what sportfishing is all about. It's also been a lifelong challenge, something you can enjoy forever.

I think it's fair to say shark fishing can be an obsession. Only after you've hooked a line-screaming mako and watched it soar into the air like a missile, or battled a hammerhead for hours until your arms wilt, will you genuinely understand and appreciate what shark fishing is all about. While you may have thought you hooked the shark, in reality it will have hooked you, in what may well become a pastime that lasts a lifetime.

MILT ROSKO

# 1

# Sharks:
# A Brief Natural
# History

**B**eauty is certainly in the eyes of the beholder; just look at the wide range of adjectives used to describe sharks. They're sleek and graceful, gliding through the water with ease. They're ugly and vicious, the bullies of the world's oceans. All true.

In the eyes of sportfishermen, the broad category that includes more than 350 species of sharks worldwide immediately presents a problem of sorts. Where anglers are accustomed to fishing for easily identified and recognizable species such as striped bass, tarpon, and wahoo, they're often stumped when it comes to distinguishing among shark species.

Even within the scientific community differences exist, particularly with the variety of local names attributed to a species; in some cases only minute nuances differentiate one from another.

*Blue sharks are among the most plentiful sharks in the oceans of the world. They regularly travel with schools of migrating fish such as mackerel, bluefish, tuna, and other forage species, as they know a ready meal is always available.*

The one thing scientists agree on is the lineage of sharks. Give or take a few million years, it's estimated the predators evolved 400 million years ago! While most of us have visions of all sharks being huge predators, the fact of the matter is that more than 75 percent of them are less than 5 feet in length at maturity.

Predators they are though, and they've done of fine job of being the housekeepers of the world's oceans. They stalk the weak and helpless and scavenge the oceans for marine life that has expired, all part of a ritual that has gone on for eons.

Unlike most fish, which have a bony skeleton, the skeleton of sharks is composed of cartilage. Also unlike fish, which have a single gill on each side of their head, sharks have five to seven pairs of gills, with a comparable number of gill clefts. Each gill vents independently into the water.

While most fish have an air bladder, sharks do not. Much of their buoyancy comes as a result of their huge liver, which often constitutes fully 25 percent of the shark's weight. The liver has a high oil content, which is lighter than water and as such provides much of the shark's buoyancy. If sharks don't continuously swim, many species of shark will simply sink, unlike many species of fish, such as the halibut and flounder, which can remain motionless on the bottom.

Sharks are noted for their rough, sandpaperlike skin. Actually it's not skin at all, but placoid scales, which give the skin its coarse feel. The placoid scales are very small and project from the shark's flesh. They're actually much like the shark's teeth, only on a tiny scale. They serve to reduce drag as a shark swims through the water.

For many years sharks were commercially harvested just for their skin. The skin is chemically treated to remove the placoid scales, resulting in a smooth skin, and then tanned much like the skins of mammals. While still done in a limited way, worldwide conservation efforts toward sharks have drastically curtailed this practice.

Shark teeth have long held a fascination throughout the world. They can be compared to snowflakes, with no two sharks having identical tooth structure. The one thing that can be stated unequivocally is that the design of shark teeth perfectly suits their purpose of seizing, impaling, and ripping or cutting through the flesh of fish and mammals. Some are even designed to crush crustaceans and mollusks.

The teeth are embedded in the gums of the shark, not the jaws as with fish. As they loosen, or are ripped free in encounters with fish or mammals, they are replaced, and a new tooth, or even a whole new set of teeth, moves forward in the gums. A study recently estimated that in a shark's lifetime it might lose upward of 30,000 teeth!

Never underestimate the vicious damage that a shark's teeth can inflict, or the power in its jaws, which clench down like a tightened vise and never relinquish their hold. Often they wildly shake their heads, ripping huge chunks of flesh from seals, sea lions, whales, porpoises, and fish of all sizes. Unsuspecting seabirds and ducks resting on the surface regularly succumb to the jaws of sharks. They're known to stalk 100-pound tarpon finning in the current beneath Florida Keys bridges, literally biting off their tails before devouring the remainder of the silver king. They commit the same mayhem on broadbill swordfish that weigh upward of 500 pounds, which often loll on the surface, basking in the sunshine, only to suddenly have their life ended in a blood-curdling slash from a huge mako or tiger shark.

Many sharks require years to reach sexual maturity. Some don't reproduce until reaching an age of 10 to 20 years and a weight of several hundred pounds. Several species live to the ripe old age of 50 years.

A limited number of oviparous shark species lay eggs, which are fertilized internally and float free. The egg cases of some have a filamentous series of threadlike organs that attach to sea grasses or algae until they hatch.

The majority of sharks are ovoviviparous: The eggs are fertilized within the female and hatch within her body. While some species produce a large number of offspring, the majority produce but a limited number, which in some instances measure 24 to 48 inches in length at birth. While still within the female some young sharks cannibalize others, reducing the birthing to but one to three of the strongest surviving offspring.

Wherever sharks are found they've often been harvested commercially for their food value, the oil from their livers, or their skin. In recent years shark fins have become increasingly popular as a basis for soups, which led to the practice of the fins being cut off live sharks and the sharks released overboard, where they eventually died. This practice has now been outlawed in the United States and other parts of the world.

While sharks have been with us for millions of years, indiscriminate harvesting will cause most shark populations to decline. Fortunately, where sportsman, including this writer, once killed sharks without giving it a second thought, many of us now work

*Years ago many charter and party boat crews set out shark baits and caught sharks like this huge specimen, which were brought to dock for display and then discarded. With the passage of time anglers realized what a wasteful practice this was, and now conservation and preservation are practiced all along the coast.*

carefully to release sharks unharmed. It's equally important that the voice of sportsmen be heard when it comes to regulating the shark fishery, particularly the commercial sector. Indiscriminate harvesting could conceivably make sharks that have survived for eons virtually extinct.

It's important that we recognize what a valuable resource the sharks of the world are, and ensure their survival in the years ahead.

# 2

# Meet the Sharks

Throughout the world scientists have identified more than 350 species of sharks. Some are contiguous to a specific area, while others are pelagic, with many traveling the waters of the world. Indeed, documentation exists of sharks crossing oceans, and moving from the North American continent to the South American continent. Many live to a ripe old age. In size they range from the tiny, 2-foot-long cat shark on up to the mammoth whale shark, which attains a length of more than 60 feet.

I suspect that at one time or another, somewhere in the world, fishermen have sought and often caught many species of sharks on sporting tackle. For the purposes of this treatise I plan on covering the sportfishing opportunities for a relative handful of sharks, including both pelagic and inshore species regularly encountered along the Atlantic, Pacific, and Gulf coasts.

It's important to note that there are few occasions when you can target a specific species of sharks with a reasonable expectation

*The majority of the most popular sharks found off the Atlantic, Pacific, and Gulf coasts can be subdued on stand-up tackle. Neal Yomans leans into an 8-foot-long bull shark while fishing off Jekyll Island, Georgia, aboard the N2 Deep. Make certain your tackle is in mint condition, for any flaw will be quickly found during a prolonged encounter with a huge shark.*

of catching it. Many different species of sharks travel together, and whether you're chumming offshore or probing inshore shallows, any one of the sharks that frequent these areas may happen upon your bait or lure. Throughout this book I'll concentrate on techniques that will succeed in the majority of situations where you're apt to encounter the shark species I've identified here, and any others that may come into range.

In more than half a century of traveling along our seacoast I've been fortunate to have tangled with a wide variety of sharks, from monster hammerheads off the Carolina Outer Banks to a long-tailed thresher off the kelp beds of the Todos Santos Islands off Ensenada, Mexico. There were brute bull sharks while sailing from Grand Isle, Louisiana, and blacktip sharks on light tackle while fishing the gorgeous reefs off Bermuda. Far offshore in the Hudson Canyon it was the thrill of a lifetime to catch a mako that came under the quartz lights of our *Linda June* as we drifted 100 miles seaward where the canyon meets the continental shelf. The list goes on, and on, each species a little different, some more formidable than others. All, however, should be truly respected for their vicious nature and the danger they present to anyone who dares to treat them carelessly.

## BLACKTIP SHARK

The blacktip shark, *Carcharhinus limbatus,* is caught on all three coasts and is among the smaller sharks encountered by anglers. It's found primarily in tropical waters, usually inshore and especially on the flats. There are reports of blacktip sharks reaching 7 feet in length, but the majority targeted by anglers range from 3 to 6 feet, weighing up to around 75 pounds. They have typical shark lines, very sleek, and are aggressive adversaries on light tackle. Their name is derived from the notable black tips of their pectoral, dorsal, anal, and caudal fins. The body has a grayish color, with a bluish back.

The current International Game Fish Association all-tackle world record for blacktip shark weighed 270 pounds, 9 ounces. It was caught by Jurgen Oeder on September 21, 1984, while fishing in Malindi Bay, Kenya.

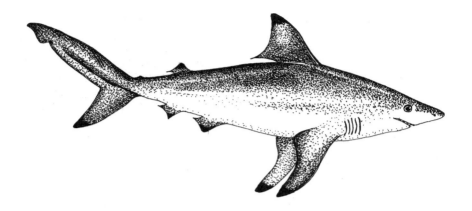

The blacktip shark has a habit of leaping from the water in a spinning motion, and as a result it's frequently confused with a spinner shark. Toward this end, confusion exists, as the spinner shark is a distinct species; even within the scientific community it's classified by different names. Regardless, the blacktip and the spinner are formidable adversaries. Typical of most sharks, they bear live young, which measure 23 to 26 inches at birth.

It appears the greatest sportfishing emphasis for blacktips occurs along the Florida Keys, where they roam the flats with such formidable game fish as bonefish, tarpon, and permit. What makes the blacktip a prized target is that it will readily strike lures, often jumping repeatedly when hooked. The key is presenting the lure as close to the shark's vision window as possible, with small plugs and leadhead jigs the most popular. Fly casters regularly score with flies such as the Honey Blonde, Lefty's Deceiver, and Half & Half patterns, using a heavy fluorocarbon tippet and short trace of fine stainless-steel or titanium leader wire to the fly.

## BLUE SHARK

In a beauty contest of sharks, the blue shark, *Prionace glauca,* would certainly dominate. Its body and back are a bright blue color, with white undersides. The color, coupled with its extra-long pectoral fins, move it through the water with casual grace. It is unquestionably the classic shark.

It has triangular, serrated teeth that slash through fish with ease, and great care should be exercised when handling one at boatside. Blue sharks measuring 8 to 12 feet in length are not uncommon, and occasional specimens upward of 15 feet are encountered offshore. The female gives birth to more than 50 young ranging up to 2 feet in length.

Joe Seidel landed the current IGFA all-tackle world-record blue shark, a 528-pound behemoth, while fishing off Montauk Point, New York, on August 9, 2001.

The blue shark is far and away one of the most common sharks, found in all the waters of the world. Blue sharks don't require large amounts of food to sustain themselves, as they are very efficient predators. Often they travel in schools, following the migration paths of species such as mackerel, bluefish, herring, and other forage. Their travels are widespread, and the scientific community has reported individual specimens traveling thousands of miles.

Where populations of edible sharks have declined in many waters of the world, blue shark populations have remained reasonably healthy. This in part may be due to the fact that the meat of the blue shark is less than desirable, having a very heavy ammonia taste, even with proper handling after being caught. Because of this many anglers view blue sharks as a fine challenge on rod and reel, and promptly release them at boatside.

## BULL SHARK

The bull shark, *Carcharhinus leucas,* frequents the waters of South America and North America and the Gulf of Mexico. In some areas it's called the cub shark. It's easily distinguished by its short, rounded snout, the lack of markings on its fins, and its very small eyes. It has a very husky body for its length, with a gray to gray-brown back and sides and nominal white underbelly.

It's one of the largest inshore sharks, often reaching a weight of 400 pounds and measuring up to 12 feet in length. An inshore species, it has somewhat triangular teeth that are serrated and can immobilize a sizable fish in an instant. It regularly feeds in shallow coastal waters and enters bays and river systems to feed on abundant forage species. It even enters fresh water in tropical areas; the deaths of many swimmers are attributed to the bull shark. It has a propensity for searching for food in the shallows, the same beaches frequented by swimmers. Here in the shallows it feeds on schooling fish such as mackerel and jacks, along with rays, skates, other sharks, and the many inshore game and food fish found in the shallows.

Its young are born in brackish water during the spring and are an impressive 28 inches long at birth.

Many scientists who track shark attacks on humans classify the bull shark as the most dangerous shark in the world. This is due to the diversity of its habitat, most of which is inshore, thus posing a

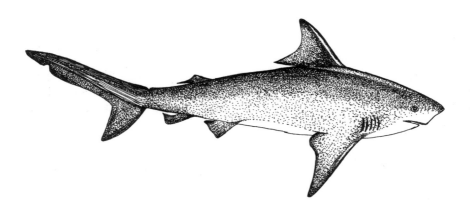

danger to man. Some attribute the bull shark's bad temper to hormonal rage. It has been determined that male bull sharks have among the highest testosterone levels of any living animal. They're said to have higher levels of testosterone than bull elephants!

The current all-tackle IGFA world record weighed an impressive 697 pounds, 12 ounces, and was caught by Ronald de Jager on March 24, 2001, while he fished the waters off Malindi in Kenya.

## DUSKY SHARK

The dusky shark, *Carcharhinus obscurus,* is considered an inshore/offshore species. Unlike the bull shark, however, which frequents the shallows, the dusky instead frequents both inshore and offshore waters, often several miles from land, along the Atlantic coast. It is particularly plentiful in the waters of Florida and along the Gulf coast. As with most sharks, it depends on a plentiful food supply, scavenging the waters for a wide variety of species.

It has a distinctive ridge on its back between the dorsal fins, with a short snout and very large pectoral fins. The dusky has a lead-colored back that occasionally has a blue tint, with a nominal white underbelly. It grows to approximately 12 feet in length, and gives birth to huge offspring that measure from 36 to 48 inches at birth.

The current IGFA all-tackle world record is represented by a huge 764-pound beauty that was landed by Warren Girle on May 28, 1982, while fishing out of Longboat Key in Florida.

## THE HAMMERHEADS

The hammerheads are included here as a family of sharks simply because they share so many similar characteristics. For our purposes, they include the bonnet shark, *Sphyrna tiburo;* the great hammerhead, *S. mokarran;* the scalloped hammerhead, *S. lewini;* and the smooth hammerhead, *S. zygaena.* These species derive their name from the distinct hammer-shaped heads they have, with one exception. The bonnet shark has a head that's shaped more like a shovel, and in fact in some areas is called a shovel head shark. The remaining hammerheads have nuances that for scientific purposes distinguish one from the other. For practical fishing purposes, their extended hammer-shaped heads, with protruding eyes, make them easy to distinguish.

The majority of hammerheads are brownish gray to light gray in color, with the smooth hammerhead leaning toward olive coloration. They're primarily a tropical species, although they're regularly encountered as far north as New England during the summer months. They give live birth to specimens ranging from 18 to 28 inches in length.

The current all-tackle IGFA world-record great hammerhead shark weighed an impressive 991 pounds. It was landed by Allen Ogle on May 30, 1982, while fishing off Sarasota, on Florida's Gulf coast.

The bonnethead shark is a lightweight and its current all-tackle IGFA world record weighed in at 23 pounds, 11 ounces. It was caught by Chad Wood on August 5, 1994, while he fished the waters of Cumberland Sound in Georgia.

The majority of hammerheads we've encountered, and subsequently caught, have been while fishing for other species. Off Miami Beach, Florida, we had a huge hammerhead engulf a swimming mullet bait being trolled for sailfish. On another occasion the biggest hammerhead we baited, a 12-foot-long specimen, was one of several sunning themselves on the surface while we trolled for blue marlin off Hatteras, North Carolina. They refused repeated passes that were made with the rigged mullet and balao baits we were using. Shutting down and drifting a whole mullet within its range of

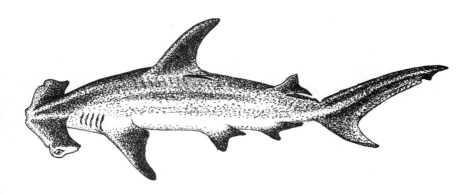

vision or scent caused one hammerhead to sink into the depths for a moment, where it quickly engulfed the mullet and proved to be an extremely tough adversary.

One of the smallest hammerheads we've encountered was while June and I were fishing for fluke, less than ½ mile off the beach at Mantoloking, New Jersey, aboard our *Linda June*. June hooked a fluke, and while reeling it in suddenly had the rod almost ripped from her grasp. Unbeknownst to us, a shark had clenched down on her fluke. The shark made repeated runs, but eventually she brought a 6-foot-long hammerhead alongside the boat. It actually wasn't hooked, but had its jaw clenched down on what was a 3-pound fluke. Thrashing at boatside, the hammerhead ripped the fluke from the hook, much to our delight, as we didn't want any part of it!

## LEOPARD SHARK

While identification of some species of sharks is very difficult because of similarities, such is not the case with the leopard shark, *Triakis semifasciata*. It's readily identified by the distinctive leopard-like markings on its body. A resident of Pacific coastal waters, it's a lightweight as sharks go, growing to a length of 7 feet, although most are smaller.

The leopard shark bears from 4 to 30 live young, which are born in inshore waters of the Pacific ranging from Oregon to the Gulf of California.

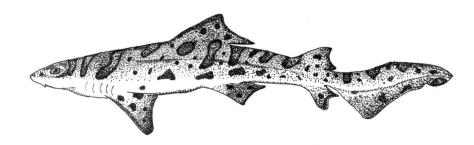

Fred Oakley landed the current all-tackle IGFA world-record leopard shark of 40 pounds, 10 ounces, while fishing off Oceanside, California, on May 13, 1994.

Sportfishermen regularly catch leopard sharks, often as an incidental catch while seeking other game and food fish. It's a shark species that's considered fine table fare by boat fishermen, but great care must be taken to promptly clean and ice its delicate meat to keep it in prime condition.

While I've been on board party boats when leopard sharks have been caught, it's one species that has eluded me. I must say that I've enjoyed viewing this and other Pacific coast sharks in Jenkinson's Aquarium in Point Pleasant, New Jersey. Anglers who have not had an opportunity to fish the Pacific are certain to enjoy the fine tank of Pacific sharks at this popular aquarium.

## LEMON SHARK

The lemon shark, *Negaprion brevirostris,* is understandably readily identified by its lemonlike, yellowish brown color. A resident of tropical waters, it has two dorsal fins of almost identical size, which is unusual in that the rear dorsal fin of most sharks is smaller than the first dorsal. Its tail is elongated, with the upper lobe much larger than the lower.

Lemon sharks frequently travel in small schools, resting on or near the bottom as they seek their prey. They're basically inshore feeders, often frequenting the same beaches as swimmers, with shark attacks having been attributed to the species. It's speculated that

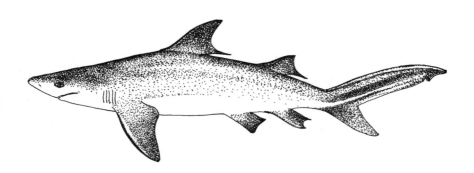

they're nocturnal feeders, spending more time feeding during hours of darkness than during daylight.

Colleen D. Harlow was fishing off Buxton, North Carolina, on November 23, 1994, when she hooked the 405-pound beauty that stands as the current all-tackle IGFA world record for lemon sharks.

They're found in all the waters of the world, caught off our Atlantic, Pacific and Gulf coasts, where they provide fine sportfishing opportunities. I've landed several that rose in chum lines dispensed over Florida reefs while we were targeting snappers and groupers. Often they're the marauder that, while you're fighting a yellowtail snapper, will grab hold, giving you a momentary thrill before departing with what might have been your dinner. A quick switch to a shark rig and live baitfish will hook the marauder.

## SHORTFIN MAKO SHARK

The shortfin mako shark, *Isurus oxyrinchus,* migrates long distances and in the eyes of most anglers who seek sharks is far and away the favorite. The mako is a beautiful, streamlined shark that moves through the water with grace. It has a cobalt color prevailing the length of its body and extending to well down its sides, where it meets a snow-white belly.

Mako sharks occasionally reach a weight of 1,000 pounds. An extremely strong pelagic shark, the mako will test an angler's skill and tackle to the utmost. It is one of the few pelagic sharks that will leap into the air when hooked, often jumping three or four times. It leaps skyward, often reaching a height of 20 feet, completely turns over, and crashes back in headfirst.

Luke Sweeney was at the right place at the right time when he hooked a big shortfin mako shark while fishing off Chatham, Massachusetts, on July 21, 2001. When finally placed on the scales it weighed an impressive 1,221 pounds, and currently is the all-tackle IGFA world record.

There is a consensus among the scientific community that worldwide mako shark populations are declining. Of all the sharks, the mako's meat commands a premium, for it has a flavor not unlike that of broadbill swordfish. This has put tremendous fishing pressure on mako stocks, by both commercial and sportfishermen.

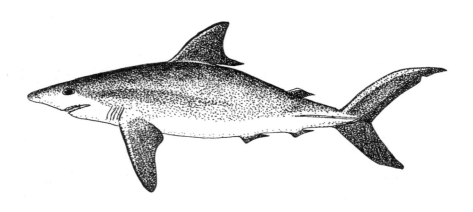

Consider for a moment that female mako sharks aren't sexually mature until they reach more than 500 pounds in weight. As the mako is ovoviviparous, its eggs develop inside the mother and from four to sixteen young are born alive. From that it's easy to understand that excessive fishing pressure and harvesting of small mako sharks has a drastic impact on the survival of the species.

It is only in recent years that we've come to understand the negative aspects of shark fishing tournaments that kill sharks, and excessive harvesting of small sharks. Both impact the shark population and warrant curtailment whenever possible. Fortunately, most tournaments now have minimum sizes.

# PORBEAGLE SHARK

The porbeagle shark, *Lamna nasus,* is often called the mackerel or bonito shark, and is found in the Atlantic off North and South America, off Africa, and in the Mediterranean Sea as well. At first glance many anglers mistake it for the shortfin mako shark, so similar is its profile, the exception being that the porbeagle generally has a greater girth than a mako of the same length. It has much the same cobalt-blue coloration as a mako, with a distinctive conical snout and white patch at the trailing edge of the first dorsal fin. When laid side by side with a mako, the porbeagle's dorsal fin is positioned farther forward than the mako's. They give live birth, with the young measuring 26 to 30 inches in length.

The current all-tackle IGFA world-record porbeagle weighed 507 pounds and was landed by Christopher Bennet while fishing Pentland Firth off Caithness, Scotland, on March 9, 1993.

Its sportfishing characteristics don't compare with the mako's, although when sought with medium-weight tackle it provides many anglers with fine sport on the offshore grounds where it's most often found. It reaches weights of more than 400 pounds, and 12 feet in length. As with most sharks, it regularly takes up residence where there is an abundance of food, for as can be appreciated, the larger members of the clan require a substantial amount of forage to satisfy their appetites.

## SANDBAR SHARK

The sandbar shark, *Carcharias plumbeus,* frequents the U.S. Atlantic coast from Maine to Florida, through the waters of Central and South America, the Mediterranean Sea, and other tropical waters including the Pacific and Indian Oceans. It's not in the heavyweight class of some sharks but still attains a formidable weight of 260 pounds and a length of 10 feet. It is the most common of the large coastal sharks along the Atlantic coast.

The current all-tackle IGFA world-record sandbar shark weighed 260 pounds and was caught by Paul Delsignore on January 2, 1989, while fishing off the Gambia coast.

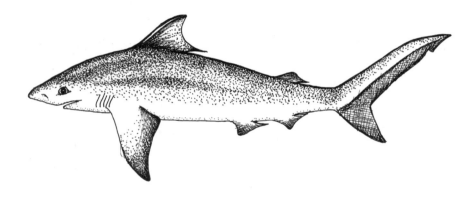

Essentially an inshore bottom feeder, it often enters the waters of bays and rivers that empty into the ocean, frequently moving into brackish water as it seeks a meal, and often causes excitement when it's observed in waters where it's not expected, or appreciated. In many areas along the coast there are small groups of anglers who target sandbar sharks, for on a medium-weight rod they'll give a good account of themselves.

It has a bluish gray-brown color with a white underside. It's by no means a spectacular adversary, but because of its weight gives a good account of itself when hooked. I've caught them quite by accident while casting from the surf of Virginia's barrier islands using menhaden as bait, and from the waters of the Chesapeake Bay while we were bottom fishing with spot as bait for black drum.

As with most sharks, it has a respectable set of dentures and must be treated with great respect. Inasmuch as they're essentially bottom feeders, the greatest majorities are caught incidentally to the species being targeted. As such the angler is often not prepared to deal with what is often a huge shark thrashing about on the sand or, even worse, brought aboard a boat. Far better to immediately cut the sandbar shark free than to risk injury.

## SILKY SHARK

The silky shark, *Carcharhinus falciformis,* derives its name from its skin, which unlike the sandpaperlike hide of most sharks is more smooth and silky. In some areas it has been fished for commercially for its skin, which is tanned. Its profile is very similar to both the dusky and sandbar sharks, with the smooth skin the major difference.

The silky shark frequents the waters of both the Atlantic and Pacific and is essentially an offshore species, where it preys on the members of the mackerel, tuna, bonito, and herring clans, along with squid, crabs, and other forage. They have an almost black coloration to their back, blending to gray sides and grayish white undersides.

The silky shark grows to 11 feet long. The females carry an average of four to six young sharks, which are 24 inches in length when born.

Bryce Robert Henderson currently holds the all-tackle IGFA world record for silky sharks with a 762-pound, 12-ounce, beauty he landed while fishing off Port Stephens, New South Wales, Australia, on February 26, 1994.

The majority of silky sharks are encountered where sportfishing or commercial fleets are targeting species such as albacore, yellowfin, or bluefin tuna, bonito, or dolphin. Many are caught on a shark rig that is set out with a fillet or chunk of bait cut from the targeted species and just drifted along.

## TIGER SHARK

Think of a tiger and you think of stripes, and when you see a tiger shark, *Galeocerdo cuvier,* you'll see that it too has stripes. The stripes are especially prominent in young tiger sharks, and sometimes might be characterized as spots or blotches as they age, often practically disappearing in large sharks.

As sharks go, the tiger shark is a heavyweight, often growing to 1,800 pounds and a length of more than 20 feet, with some reportedly reaching 30 feet. *Ferocious* is a word that aptly describes this brute of a shark, which because of its very size is a challenge to sportfishermen. Often called a man-eater, there are numerous reports of tiger sharks attacking humans. It's found in far-offshore waters but also frequents the shallows along beaches frequented by swimmers. They are particularly plentiful where there is a large turtle population, as they feed extensively on them. As with most shark attacks on humans, there is a consensus that the tiger shark mistakenly strikes a swimming human in the belief that it's a prey.

Little did Walter Maxwell realize that when a big tiger shark took his bait while fishing off Cherry Grove, South Carolina, he'd eventually land an all-tackle IGFA world record. It was June 14, 1964, when he hooked the brute, which back at the dock pulled the scale down to an impressive 1,780 pounds.

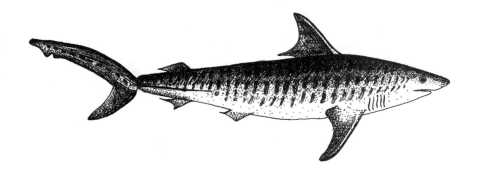

As with most sharks, tiger sharks take up what I call an opportunistic residency whenever schools of smaller fish are located. They're notorious for being in an area where huge schools of bluefin tuna, yellowfin tuna, bonito, and other forage are located. I've caught them fishing the grounds 45 miles southeast of Montauk Point, New York, while we chummed for bluefin tuna but had the foresight to put out a shark rig, which not only accounted for a tiger but over a period of several years brought me other species as well, including blue sharks, the common thresher, and makos.

## THE THRESHER SHARKS

There are several species of thresher sharks you're apt to encounter when fishing offshore waters. As a family the threshers are easily distinguished from other sharks, for their sicklelike tails are approximately as long as their body. The common thresher, *Alopias vulpinus,* is a more inshore species; the most popular, reaching 20 feet in length and 1,000 pounds in weight; it's a formidable adversary.

The current IGFA all-tackle world-record thresher weighed in at 767 pounds, 3 ounces, and was hooked on February 26, 1983, by D. L. Hannah while fishing Bay of Islands, New Zealand.

Where some species of sharks have very specific and distinct coloration, such is not the case with the thresher family, as their color ranges from brown to blue, gray, and almost black, in varying degrees, with an overall tint of slate.

The common thresher and others in its clan give live birth, with the young measuring 30 to 48 inches at birth. As with most sharks, common threshers congregate wherever forage is available and feed extensively in far-offshore waters on squid, bonito, mackerel, herring, and tuna.

The Atlantic bigeye thresher shark, *Alopias superciliosus,* is often confused with the common thresher, as the only noticeable difference is its larger eyes and head with deep grooves on top. Less frequently encountered than the common thresher, the bigeye thresher is felt to spend most of its life in deep offshore waters. The Pacific bigeye thresher shark, *A. profundis,* has much the same characteristics as its Atlantic cousin, spending its life in far-offshore waters, often in the depths. Both species are considered a rare catch, and are less frequently encountered than the common thresher.

Many consider the threshers on a par with mako sharks as far as eating quality is concerned. They have a flavor much like broadbill swordfish, making them a prize catch of both sport- and commercial fishermen. As with mako sharks, anglers are cautioned to limit their catch of this fine, slow-growing game fish, for overexploitation can severely impact their abundance.

## WHITE SHARK

The white shark, *Carcharodon carcharias,* is the shark that was made famous in the movie *Jaws.* Called man-eater and great white shark, this is the granddaddy of sharks, with specimens reported that were

25 feet in length. Conservation efforts have recognized that the population of white sharks is very limited, and there is, to my knowledge, no targeted fishery for them. I've included it in this compilation because of the fascination anglers and the general population have with this humongous shark that may reach up to 2 tons in weight!

In more than half a century of offshore fishing I've encountered white sharks on three occasions. The first was while returning from an offshore tuna trolling rip. In the distance we could see clouds of seagulls, and investigation disclosed the carcass of a huge whale floating on the surface. As we approached, its smell was sickening. Several small sharks leisurely swam around the perimeter of the whale's huge body.

As we moved in to the other side of the whale the water erupted. It was a great white shark, literally biting off chunks of blubber, thrashing its head viciously as it ripped pieces the size of a bushel basket from the whale.

A conservative estimate put its length at close to 20 feet. What was awesome was the girth of the great white, which appeared to be quadruple that of any other shark I'd ever seen. It was Mother Nature at her finest, with the great white and accompanying blue sharks keeping the ocean's waters clean. We never gave a thought to trying to catch it.

Just a couple of years later we were aboard the *Linda June,* our first boat, a 24-foot Wellcraft Airslot with twin Mercruiser stern drives, and about to return from the waters off Block Island where we'd made a nice catch of codfish. There was a gentle swell, and we began to leisurely head back to Montauk, when a huge white shark—it appeared almost as long as the boat—ran parallel with us not more than a dozen feet from where I stood at the helm. Its length and girth were awesome, and it swam with us for several hundred feet, an absolutely beautiful sight. It gave me the same rush that I feel to this day.

The final sighting came when aboard our second *Linda June,* a 33-foot Bertram. We were trolling at Hudson Canyon along the edge of the continental shelf, close to 100 miles offshore, and

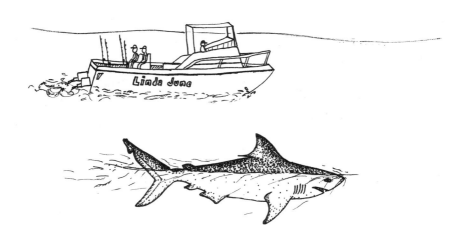

enjoying a great day with yellowfin tuna. It was then that a big white shark, again close to 20 feet long, swam by as we were jockeying in and out of gear while fighting a pair of yellowfins. It never did bother the tuna; I suspect it had already had its fill. Still, it gave us pause, as it too swam perilously close, wondering what we were doing in its domain.

The current all-tackle IGFA world record was established way back on April 21, 1959, by Alfred Dean. He hooked the 2,664-pound brute while fishing off Ceduna, South Australia.

## WHITETIP SHARK

The whitetip shark, *Carcharhinus longimanus,* is an offshore species, seldom moving inside of the 100-fathom line. It's a tropical shark that has a very distinctive round snout, with rounded dorsal and pectoral fins, usually with white mottling on tips. It's very broad for its length, and among the huskier sharks. As with so many sharks, its coloration varies, perhaps due to the waters it frequents and its diet. They range from light brown to blue across the back, blending to a pale off-white underside.

Whitetip sharks reach a length of 13 feet and will exceed 400 pounds. They're found in far-offshore waters of both the Atlantic and Pacific Oceans, and give birth to 2 to 10 live young measuring 27

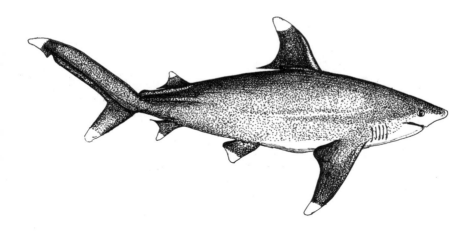

inches in length. While not considered as formidable an adversary as other sharks, their sheer size makes them tough to bring to boatside.

The majority of whitetip sharks spend their time traveling with schools of bluefin tuna, yellowfin tuna, albacore, bonito, and mackerel, where any straggler becomes fair game. Many whitetip sharks are hooked while anglers are chumming for members of the tuna clan, but on shark rigs that are set to capitalize on the fact they're known to travel with the tuna schools.

## OTHER SHARKS

Included here has been a representative grouping of sharks that are among the favorites of sportfishermen. There's quite a challenge, for you'll require a capable boat, along with a substantial amount of quality equipment and tackle, to seek out the world-ranging sharks, coaxing them to strike a bait or lure, and have the skill and physical tenacity to bring them to boatside.

Some sharks were not included because of their limited range. One such shark is the salmon shark. It is found in the waters off Alaska to southern California, where it forages on the salmon population, among other fish species, and provides fine sport for that state's anglers. Recognizing its potential as a game fish, Alaska has restricted commercial fishing for it.

Each species has its unique characteristics. It's actually surprising that scientists have done their research and uncovered the unusual habits of various sharks. Just recently, while researching some of the technical aspects of this book, I learned of the sleeper shark. This toothsome critter is like the ocean's vacuum cleaner, sometimes feeding on the bottom more than a mile deep, where it devours decaying fish and mammals. The decaying matter emits a scent that can be identified by the sleeper shark from a mile away. Once it has its fill and its stomach is to the bursting point, it reportedly does not have to eat for a month at a time!

The deeper you become involved in shark fishing, the more you'll come to enjoy it; there's always something to learn. Just the ability to identify the sharks you catch will be a challenge, and there'll always be surprises when you catch a species you didn't expect to be in the area. They're all a challenge, make no mistake about it, and in the following chapter I'll detail the tackle and techniques that can enable you to make many fine catches of these great game fish.

# 3

# Basic Shark Tackle

Today's shark anglers are afforded the opportunity of heading seaward in search of their favorite game fish with the finest fishing equipment ever made, and at a price unheard of just a few years ago. Technology has played an important role in the development of rods, reels, and lines, the three components of your basic shark outfit. The key is in deciding which outfit is best for you.

For purposes of this chapter I'll deal with three basic outfits built to target the big sharks, most of which are pelagic and roam the waters of the world. In a later chapter the lighter tackle for inshore sharks, where casting tackle is appropriate, will be covered as it applies to the smaller members of the shark family.

Big-game tackle designed for the heavyweights of the shark clan includes offshore trolling tackle, stand-up tackle, and ultralight stand-up tackle. By far the two most popular types are offshore

*The author displays the basic tackle he employs while seeking sharks, including a 30-pound-class stand-up outfit, Snap Float, and whole mackerel bait. The rod belt and kidney harness enable him to move about the cockpit with ease while going toe-to-toe with a big shark.*

trolling—which as its name implies is used for trolling but often serves double duty when chumming—and stand-up tackle, which is designed for stand-up fishing and generally lighter in weight and easier to handle than trolling tackle. Its shorter rod length has the advantage of exerting more leverage on a shark, but on the negative side it doesn't have the length to hold a shark away from the boat or work it under the stern in a crisis. Ultralight stand-up tackle had its beginnings on the long-range boats that sail from southern California ports and target primarily big tuna. Anglers found the traditional rods, reels, and lines were somewhat cumbersome when fishing from long-range party boats. They designed complete outfits so they would be extremely light in weight, enabling an angler to fight a fish for an hour or two's duration yet not be fatigued by the weight of the outfit. Designing these outfits was made possible in great part by the advent of Spectra braided lines and other equally fine-diameter lines. These newer lines literally tripled the line capacity of smaller-sized reels, resulting in a perfect marriage that accomplished the objective of both light weight and the strength and power of graphite rods, to subdue not only tuna and marlin but also many of the powerful pelagic sharks.

## TROLLING RODS

Within the framework of the offshore trolling category used by shark anglers are rods rated for 30-, 50-, 80-, and 130-pound-class tackle. The rods are designed for use while fighting sharks from a fighting chair. They are equipped with either a straight or a curved butt of a length that is easily accommodated when an angler uses a bucket harness and sits in a fighting chair.

Many offshore trolling rods are built by small custom rod shops, with wrappings designed to match the angler's boat colors, name, and personal preference. The major manufacturers also produce rods of fine quality, including Penn, Daiwa, Shimano, Loomis, and Lamiglas.

The majority of these rods, irrespective of the line test rating, measure from 6 feet to 7 feet, 6 inches, in overall length. The tip sections are made of fiberglass or graphite, or are hybrids that combine the best attributes of each in making a powerful tip section.

The tip sections usually have five or six roller guides and a roller tip-top. The roller guides permit the line to pass over the rollers with minimal pressure, reducing the likelihood of line failure due to abrasion after a long fight with a big shark. Roller guides perform flawlessly when properly cared for. It's incumbent upon you to regularly lubricate them so they literally roll, ensuring smooth performance during a long encounter with a big shark.

*Mustad manufactures the largest shark hook made, a 19/0 with a piece of chain, which is used with big baits such as this little tunny. This is appropriate when seeking really big sharks and using heavy tackle in the 80- or 130-pound class.*

Today's rod guides are most often double-wrapped with nylon thread, including custom designs for your particular taste or boat. The wrappings should be sealed with an epoxy finish, resulting in a rod that will give many years of service.

The tip section is also fitted with a comfortable foregrip. Some are made of cork or felt-covered cork; there are also the newer synthetic, high-density foam grips. Look for models that have a 10- to 12-inch-long foregrip, as opposed to some that are only half that length. The longer length enables you to adjust your grasp to maximize your comfort level, especially important during a long fight.

The butt sections of the majority of trolling rods are made of aluminum, with a gimbal that fits the fighting chair. The reel seats have a female ferrule into which a screw-locking male ferrule of the tip section fits. The reel seat also has a screw-locking feature to hold the reel securely in place. Toward this end, always employ a strap wrench to both tighten and loosen the screw-locking feature, to secure the tip section as well as the reel. Hand-tightening just won't work, and with the tremendous pressure brought to bear when fighting a big shark you just don't want the tip or reel to come loose.

With outfits ranging from 30- to 50-pound class, most anglers employ straight butts, although bent butts are also available should you prefer this feature, which enables you to maximize pressure when fighting a shark. When you move up to 80- or 130-pound class tackle, a bent butt is a good choice, as with such heavy gear you're of necessity fighting all fish from the fighting chair.

## TROLLING REELS

Reels used for offshore trolling are classified with the same designations as rods, with those ranging from 30- to 130-pound class most appropriate for offshore shark fishermen. For many years the vintage Penn Senator reels, equipped with star drags, were the standard on the offshore scene and regularly accounted for many fine shark catches. To this day they're made to the same strict quality standards as established by Otto Henze, the company founder, and are well within the range of shark fishermen who must go forth with a limited budget for tackle selection.

At the other end of the reel spectrum is Fin-Nor, whose throw-lever drag reels filled the top-of-the-line niche for many years, with excellent engineering and big-game reels well up to the challenge of the largest sharks. Indeed, for a period of many years the Penn Senator and Fin-Nor dominated the market.

Beginning in the mid-1960s Penn introduced its International Series, which big-game fishermen welcomed with open arms as an engineering marvel within the financial reach of most offshore anglers. The "gold reels," as they came to be known, combined precision engineering, durability, and functional design to provide anglers seeking tuna, marlin, sharks, and other game fish with a reel that became the standard for four decades.

The Internationals featured a one-piece machined gold-anodized frame, supersmooth drag washers powered by a lever-drag mechanism, and shielded stainless-steel ball bearings. The stainless-steel, machine-cut main gears, pinion gears, and drag cams provided a quality that was unsurpassed in saltwater reels.

The second-generation Internationals provided two-speed capability with a push-button shifting system whereby the angler has the choice of high-speed retrieve or power retrieve when pumping a stubborn fish.

*Sharks just never give up, especially when brought to boatside. Tackle and equipment must always be kept in mint condition if you want to consistently land the heavyweights.*

With the passage of time many other reels entered the offshore scene, including quality products by Shimano, Daiwa, and Tiagra. In the high-end range, reels made by Accurate and Duel established a standard that is difficult to beat. The Accurate is the first big-game reel to have drags on both sides of the spool. This disperses the drag friction over the surface of two drag plates instead of just one, resulting in a much smoother drag and longer life for the drag washers.

The Accurate incorporates five stainless-steel ball bearings, resulting in incredible free spool and remarkable smoothness under a heavy load, especially important with the larger models used for fighting big sharks.

Not to be outdone, Duel's engineers have made several remarkable innovations in big-game reels. Their double-speed reels use an automatic shift system, negating the use of a button to change speed. For speed reeling, when taking up slack on a charging shark, for example, the angler simply reels by turning the handle clockwise. For power, required when pumping a stubborn shark from the depths, the handle is cranked in reverse, or counterclockwise. Once you develop the rhythm, it's relatively easy.

Another innovation with the Duel is gears that are completely sealed within an oil bath, which ensures reliability during a long, heat-generating fight. The reel's spool includes its own drag rings and springs. By changing the number of springs, you get different drag capabilities for different line sizes.

## ROD-AND-REEL COMBOS

By now you may be in a quandary as to which rod-and-reel combo would be best suited to your needs as you head offshore to seek sharks. From a practical point of view you've got to build into the equation whether you'll be fishing for other big-game fish such as marlin, tuna, wahoo, and dolphin. In that way you'll equip your boat with a selection that can be used for a variety of fishing opportunities, recognizing that there's a limit as to just how many outfits it's practical to have on board.

*With the reel in free spool and its audible click on, a homemade clothespin clip holds the line secure as you anticipate a strike. When a shark takes the bait, the line snaps free, enabling the shark to move off unimpeded and permitting you to remove the rod from the holder, lock the reel in gear, and strike the shark.*

Included below is what I'd term the average line capacities, gear ratios, and weights of the most popular, wide-spool offshore big-game reels:

| LINE CLASS | LINE CAPACITY IN YARDS | GEAR RATIO | REEL WEIGHT IN OUNCES |
|---|---|---|---|
| 30 | 900/30 | 3.8:1 | 59 |
| 50 | 850/50 | 3:1 | 67.5 |
| 80 | 950/80 | 2.7:1 | 85.5 |
| 130 | 950/130 | 2.2:1 | 195 |

These outfits are balanced, in that the total outfit is capable of exerting maximum drag pressure with the respective lines being used. It's important to note that many shark fishermen feel there's really no need to spool 900 yards on a reel. The thinking is that if a shark is capable of ripping 2,700 feet of line from a reel, without the boat having been brought into play to support the angler's efforts, then the shark—or any other game fish—deserves to get away!

Using this logic, many anglers load their 30-pound-class reels with 50-pound-test line, their 50-pound-class reels with 80-pound-test line, their 80-pound-class reels with 130-pound-test line, and their 130-pound-class reels with 200-pound-test line. While this reduces the amount of line you can spool on a specific reel, many anglers feel that the heavier line enables them to bring more pressure to bear, and understandably, the heavier the line, the less chance there is of abrasion, knot failure, or a line break.

## LINE FOR TROLLING

Among shark fishermen using the outfits just described for offshore trolling, the majority employ monofilament line, although there are devotees of Dacron as well. Because you're dealing with extremely big sharks at times, you've got to use dependable, quality lines produced by manufacturers that have been in the business and have a sterling reputation for their products. Among the premier monofilament manufacturers are Ande, Sufix, Momoi, Stren, and Jinkai. Cortland and Marlin Braid are the standard when it comes to Dacron.

Among the qualities you want to look for in a line are fine diameter, minimal stretch, and abrasion resistance. Monofilament lines are available in a variety of colors, including pink, green, blue, and white. The new high-visibility yellow lines have grown in popularity in recent years, for, as their name implies, you can clearly see them from the bridge. This make for ease in knowing exactly where your line is while trolling or fighting a shark.

If you're attempting to set an IGFA world record, make certain you select a line that states its breaking strength is at or below the stated test of the line. Toward this end, there are many lines on the market boasting that the breaking strength exceeds the rated test of the line. Using such line disqualifies you for a record, for the sample of the line you're obliged to supply when applying for the record will test beyond its rating when tested by IGFA.

Some anglers add an extra, heavy top shot of line at the terminal end instead of doubling the line. This is accomplished by splicing monofilament to Dacron, or using a loop-to-loop connection. Commercially made top shots feature small-diameter Spectra leader loops, low-profile Spectra thread serves, and double-wall loop construction. The top-shot type of terminal end results in a wind-on leader, negating the use of a ball-bearing swivel and coastlock snap to connect the trolling lure or bait. However, with shark fishing necessitating the use of wire or cable leader material, many anglers use a top shot of heavy leader—for example, a 100-pound-test top shot with 50-pound-test line, followed by a Sampo ball-bearing swivel and coastlock snap, and finally the wire or cable leader. It's also important to note that many top shots, because of their length and test, will not enable you to establish an IGFA record.

The examples of line capacity for the various-sized reels are of monofilament and Dacron line, and vary among manufacturers with

*The author prefers 30-pound-class tackle when shark fishing, and employs a Penn International 30VSW reel and matching rod. He spools 50-pound-test line on the reel, which is more than ample for most shark encounters.*

respect to both the reels and the lines. As a rule anglers do not spool Spectra and other fine-diameter lines on their big reels. However, a growing number of anglers have taken to using 20- and 30-pound-class reels, onto which they spool upward of 900 yards of 80-pound-test Spectra. This is possible because of the fine-diameter Spectra, such as Power Pro, which the author uses and provides the angler an opportunity to use a lighter reel, which makes for more enjoyable sport yet includes a tremendous amount of line on the reel. High-quality big-game reels, providing they are properly maintained and lubricated, and their drag washers regularly checked, have thus far been up to the task. Reel maintenance is extremely important. If the reel is not properly lubricated and the drag washers show signs of wear, there's a good chance of a failure during a prolonged battle with a big shark. The heat generated by long, fast runs literally melts some lubricants, and drag washers quickly show excess wear when subjected to the light reels and maximum drag pressure.

## TROLLING ACCESSORIES

Salt can play havoc with big-game reels. For serious anglers it's wise to invest in reel covers, which are placed over the reels when traveling to and from the fishing grounds. The covers are made of polyurethane-coated nylon cloth and padded with closed-cell foam. They're placed on the reel and secured with Velcro closures. By having the reels covered, you prevent salt spray—often encountered when traveling on a windswept ocean—from entering the reel's housing, where its corrosive action wreaks havoc with even the finest-quality components.

I'd recommend also having safety lines attached to each outfit you're fishing in a rod holder. Often as a shark strikes it is peeling line from the reel at an unbelievable speed, and as you attempt to remove the rod from a rod holder the outfit can be literally ripped from your hand and lost overboard. The safety line should be long enough so that as the outfit is removed from the rod holder, you can move to any location in the cockpit without being impeded because of its length. Commercially made models range in length from 10 to 15 feet and are made of ⁵⁄₁₆-inch twisted nylon spliced into a spring-loaded stainless-steel clip that is attached to the reel, with a loop at the other end. That is secured to a stern cleat or the pedestal of the fighting chair.

Many anglers employ a braided rope doughnut onto which they secure their safety lines. The doughnut is made of ¾-inch twisted nylon rope and slipped over the pedestal of the fighting chair in the cockpit. A stainless-steel clip is then placed in the loop of the safety line and snapped to the doughnut. Aboard the *Linda June* we often trolled with six or eight lines, all of which were secured in this manner. Admittedly, this was accomplished only after a brand-new 50-pound-class outfit was lost overboard when a helpful angler attempted to obtain a bucket of seawater and inadvertently knocked the outfit out of a rod holder!

## STAND-UP TACKLE

Stand-up rods and reels are designed to be used while standing up and fishing while wearing a rod belt and shoulder harness, as opposed to fighting sharks from a fighting chair. Because you're holding the rod and reel, it almost immediately rules out using 80- or 130-pound-class tackle, simply because of the outfit's weight.

This means that the majority of sharkers who use stand-up tackle use either 30- or 50-pound-class tackle. If you look at the weight of a basic 30-pound-class reel you'll find it's around 59 ounces; a 50-pound-class reel is 67½ ounces.

The most advanced reel I've begun using in my sharking excursions is the Penn International V Series two-speed reel. I've gone down to the 30-pound-class reel, on which I'm able to load almost 600 yards of 50-pound-test monofilament line. I mount it on a Penn International stand-up rod that's rated for 50- to 100-pound-test line.

Stand-up rods are built along much the same lines as offshore trolling rods, except that they have shorter tip sections, somewhat longer foregrips, and shorter butts. My favorite measures 5 feet, 6 inches, in length and has a relatively light tip section yet tremendous lifting power throughout the balance of the rod. The maximum length for a stand-up rod is about 6 feet overall.

Its short butt section, when inserted in a rod belt, puts the reel in a position where my hands naturally fall into place on the reel. If I feel my arms getting weary while I'm fighting a big shark, I can simply let go of the rod and reel, and it hangs perfectly in position from me, with the butt in the rod belt and the reel held securely in place with the straps of the shoulder harness. It feels comfortable, and that's so important when you're selecting an outfit.

This outfit feels as light as a feather, and when I wear a shoulder harness and fighting belt I feel totally relaxed. I have a great comfort level that should I hook a big mako, thresher, or tiger, I can exert pressure until the engines are started and the boat can be used to keep me in range of the fish.

What I especially like about the International V reel is that it's very compact and has a Bio-Drive Retrieve System that combines an ergonomic frame and handle design with a convenient push-button shifting system that enables me to switch from fast-speed to power retrieve in an instant. Most important, however, is a smooth-as-silk drag system. I can apply drag pressure that was never really intended for a 30-pound-class reel, but that when coupled with the stand-up rod gives me a tremendous amount of stopping power when a shark takes off for the horizon. The system features a very long 150-degree quadrant for free spool, and has a unique strip drag position that is nice when a shark picks up a bait in the chum line.

Admittedly, when I was younger I regularly employed a 50-pound outfit while stand-up sharking. Having passed the 70-year mark, I find the 30-pound outfit feels like a feather. While it may take me a little longer to land a shark than it would with a heavier outfit, I'm not at all fatigued. Before you decide on which outfits to use, might I suggest you strap on a 50-pound outfit and practice pumping in a 5-gallon pail of seawater with a couple of hundred feet of line out. Then try the same with a 30-pound outfit. I think you'll agree the lighter outfit has its advantages. Take care, however, that you've a good crew on board, as there's no room for mistakes when using the lighter outfit.

The 30-pound-class outfit has its shortcomings. Certainly I'm not physically up to putting 30 or 40 pounds of drag pressure on the reel in an attempt to stop a shark. It's just beyond my physical capability. But for the younger set, the 50-pound gear may be a better way to go.

I must emphasize, whether you're equipping your boat with offshore trolling gear or stand-up tackle, that you take your time and select matched outfits. I've been aboard boats where owners spent close to a million dollars for their craft, yet had cockpits cluttered with tackle that looked as though it came from a garage sale. Star drag reels, throw-lever reels, two-speed reels, trolling rods and stand-up rods . . . it was a hodgepodge that made you have to think when you received a strike and picked up an outfit.

I always have matched outfits, so that even if blindfolded I can concentrate on the shark and not have to fumble, and wish I were using a different outfit. I recognize that it's not always possible to

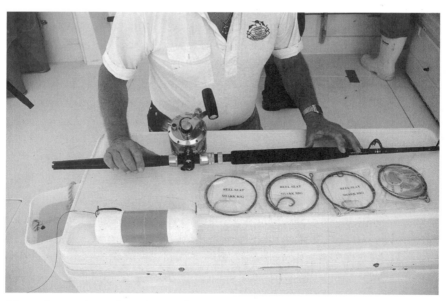

*The author employs a basic setup utilizing four basic terminal leaders made by the Reel Seat in Brielle, New Jersey, along with a Snap Float to set the desired depths and a Penn International 30VSW loaded with 50-pound-test monofilament line and matching stand-up rod.*

totally equip your boat with matched outfits if you're just beginning. But as you expand your equipment I'd suggest avoiding always trying to get the newest model on the market. Begin by selecting a quality rod, reel, and line by reputable manufacturers, and simply keep adding to it until you've got a spiffy cockpit full of matched, perfectly functioning outfits. If your budget can handle it, by all means go with the newest two-speed big-game reels. You'll never regret it.

Once you get used to stand-up tackle, you'll quickly become a devotee, as did I. Now I not only use it while chumming for sharks but also press the outfit into service while trolling and have used it while reef fishing and deep-water bottom fishing. Importantly, what makes the outfit so enjoyable to use is its light weight with superb lifting power, a combination that makes for extremely enjoyable handling of big fish, especially sharks, where you may be getting a workout over a period of an hour or more.

## ULTRALIGHT TACKLE

Ultralight stand-up tackle differs from the two basic outfits just described in that it's designed specifically to maximize the new technology of fishing tackle. I've used it on many occasions and certainly feel it's capable and effective in subduing sharks, even those weighing 200 pounds and more. Most often veteran anglers employ this gear. Its beginning came aboard the California long-range party boats, where each angler owns and maintains his own tackle. Most have spent many years at it, beginning with heavier gear that understandably is more functional for a newcomer, but graduating to gear that just didn't exist a few years ago.

The name that has stuck to these rods is *long-range casting,* as they measure 6 feet, 6 inches, in overall length and have seven or eight Fuji silicon carbide guides mounted on the lightweight yet very powerful graphite blanks. They're equipped with Aftco reel seats and gimbals, and have a very long foregrip. They're rated for 30- to 50-pound-class line and have the backbone to cast a 4- to 6-ounce lure or bait. Anytime a shark cruises within range it's relatively easy to place a live bait or chunk within its line of vision.

The reel of choice for making a balanced outfit is the Shimano Trinidad, Calcutta, or Accurate Boss. These are basically casting reels with a monofilament line capacity of approximately 420 yards of 17-pound test on the smaller models, and ranging up to a respectable 400 yards of 30-pound test on the larger models. The Trinidad has a remarkable 6.2:1 retrieve ratio, which means you can really pick up line quickly once your shark begins to tire. Equally remarkable is that these reels range in weight from 14 to 20 ounces, which makes the combination of rod, reel, and line feel like a feather in your hands, yet packs an awesome punch.

The key in using these reels is that most of the fellows who use them for shark fishing fill their spools with Spectra line, usually 50- but sometimes 80-pound test, which equates to a line capacity in excess of 500 yards. This combination results in a deadly outfit in the hands of an experienced angler.

Unlike the reels designed for offshore trolling or stand-up fishing as described earlier, they do not have harness lugs, and as such the only support come by placing the rod's gimbal butt in the rod belt, which relieves pressure somewhat while you fight a big shark. You've got to be in good shape, however, when you move into these powerful, lightweight outfits and suddenly find yourself attached to a shark of awesome proportions!

My observation has been that shark fishermen go through a period when they begin with the heavy outfits and are targeting big sharks. They then go through a phase when they gear down to stand-up tackle, content to slug it out with whatever size of shark happens by. Eventually they wind up going to the lighter gear, which, after they've built a confidence level, enables them to tough it out with all but the biggest of sharks.

Admittedly, you could be fishing with a light outfit loaded with fine Spectra line and hook the shark of a lifetime and see it spool you. But that's what memories are made of. It all adds to the fun, which is what shark fishing is all about in the first place.

# 4

# Other Equipment

I t has been said that preparation is the key to success, and that certainly is true with shark fishing. It becomes especially important when your quest of sharks may take you 100 miles or more seaward. You can't just run down to the corner tackle shop for something you forgot!

The items of equipment discussed in this chapter are all important, and as such they're discussed in no particular order, other than to say that should you forget one, it may be just the piece of gear that makes the difference between landing or losing a big mako or hammerhead.

## FIGHTING CHAIRS

Regardless of what size of boat you fish from, some sort of big-game fighting chair is helpful. This is particularly true when you're targeting pelagic sharks, many of which range up to 500 pounds or more and require a great deal of time, sometimes hours, to bring alongside.

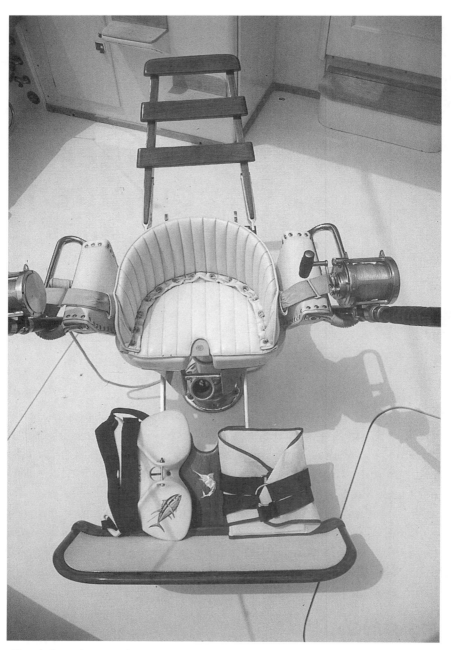

*Aboard the author's* Linda June *there was a fighting chair in the cockpit, which accommodated 30- and 50-pound-class outfits, and a bucket harness for fighting sharks from the chair. A rod belt and kidney harness were available for stand-up fishing.*

The handful of manufacturers that specialize in these chairs for the most part have top-quality products. It's preferable that you select a chair with a footrest, as this enables you to comfortably position your legs and use a sliding, back-and-forth rocking motion to methodically pump a big shark from the depths.

Most fighting chairs have a removable back, which, when it's removed, doesn't restrict your pumping action as you're fighting a shark. The majority of fighting chairs have cushioned armrests, with two built-in rod holders in each of the arms. It's extremely important that the heavy-duty pedestal of the fighting chair can be properly mounted on the deck of the cockpit, with heavy-duty support to enable through-bolting.

I've observed owners of small boats who failed to realize there was inadequate support beneath their pedestal's mounting hardware. They secured the pedestal with screws, which simply rip free when any degree of pressure is applied, a major safety concern.

While we had full-sized fighting chairs aboard the last two boats carrying the *Linda June* name, on our first boat, the 24-footer, there just wasn't room in the cockpit for a big chair. While we gave consideration to the possibility to mounting one atop the motor box, we felt it would be impractical having to remove it for access to the engines. We thought about putting one forward as well, which we've seen work well with a medium-sized chair. Instead we opted for a pair of chairs of rotocast, one-piece foam-filled polyethylene with aluminum hardware and stainless-steel fasteners. They each had a pair of comfortable cushions.

The chairs were mounted in the cockpit, between the matching helm seats and the motor box. They had a single rod holder and a gimbal; while not as comfortable as a big chair, they were just fine when tangling with most sharks. On that boat we often used stand-up tackle, and used the chair for a respite when we had a particularly stubborn shark in the depths. Because of its close proximity to the motor box, we often used it as our footrest!

## GAFFS

If you're like me, and like an increasing contingent of sharkers on all three coasts, you're likely to be releasing the majority of the sharks that are brought to boatside. However, it's recognized that from time to time anglers want to bring aboard a shark for the dinner table, and doing so will require the same amount of gear as were you boating all of them.

The flying gaff is one of the most useful and effective pieces of equipment you'll need to subdue a big shark. The design of a flying gaff, which has a barbed gaff hook, enables you to gaff a shark, after which the gaff head, which is attached to a length of nylon line, separates from the gaff handle. This results in the gaffed shark being impaled on the gaff head at the end of the rope, which makes bringing it to boatside much easier.

Before proceeding, let me state that straight gaffs have their place when landing a shark, but they're no substitute for flying gaffs.

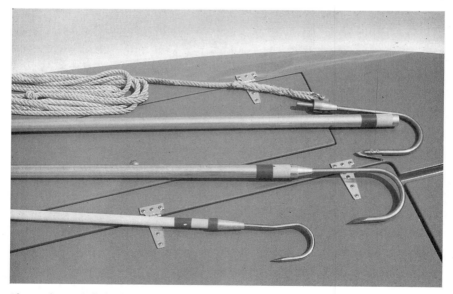

*If you plan to kill sharks, it's wise to carry several gaffs on board. Once the flying gaff is secured into the shark, the straight gaff should then be used to help position a rope to the shark's tail, tying the shark along the transom for the trip back to port. As a safety consideration, avoid bringing the shark aboard.*

Almost any respectable shark will literally rip a straight gaff from the hands of the most formidable and strong person who's handling it. Hence the importance of at least one, preferably two, flying gaffs on board.

Standard flying gaffs are generally available in 4-, 6-, and 8-inch hook sizes. Heavy-duty, double-strength gaff heads measuring 8 and 10 inches are also available, and the 8-inch model is an excellent choice for the majority of sharks you're apt to encounter. Most gaff heads are made with a fixed barb, which holds a shark securely. Some manufacturers produce a gaff head with a folding barb, which makes penetration easier. Once the gaff is implanted, the barb opens, holding the shark securely and preventing the hook from ripping out.

The flying gaff handles are 8 feet long, although 10-foot models are available from many manufacturers. The handles are either a twist lock or straight slot release; models are also available with a release mechanism that is depressed with your thumb after the gaff is planted.

I prefer to have a 20-foot-long piece of ½-inch nylon rope spliced to my flying gaff heads, with a large spliced loop at the other end. Many anglers loop the nylon rope to a stern cleat. This enables them to gaff a shark and comfortably handle the rope from the corner of the cockpit. The ½-inch rope is far superior to the ¼-inch rope that comes with some flying gaffs, as its heavier diameter is easier on the hands. Toward this end, always make certain to wear heavy-duty gloves when handling the rope. More on gloves later.

Rather than attach the flying gaff's rope to a stern cleat, I much prefer to loop it around the pedestal of the fighting chair. This enables me to move to any position in the cockpit. I can follow the person who is handling the leader wire, and I'm never impeded as I move to any position in the cockpit, on the port or starboard side, or along the transom.

If you're really into sharking, I'd recommend a pair of flying gaffs, as on occasion you'll get a green shark at boatside and, in the excitement of trying to plant the gaff, may in a split second miss targeting its head area. Thus, with the gaff in its middle, the shark becomes increasing difficult to get under control. A backup flying gaff can then be properly positioned as near to the head as possible.

This is when a straight gaff comes into play. A 6-inch gaff with an 8-foot handle is ideal. After the flying gaff rope has been used to bring the shark close astern, the straight gaff is used to secure the tail, so that a tail rope may loop around the shark's tail and secure it tight astern.

## GUNS

Over the years I've been aboard boats where a stun gun was used to subdue sharks. As a shark is brought alongside the stun gun, which is screwed to the end of an 8-foot-long handle and loaded with a shotgun shell, the gun is fired as it makes contact with the shark's body. Years ago this was a common practice, but it's now outlawed by the International Game Fish Association for record purposes, and it is seldom used today. I always found these uncomfortable to be around, and would never have one aboard one of my boats.

Many shark fishermen carry shotguns, rifles, or handguns aboard to subdue sharks, but I strongly recommend against it. Trying to shoot a thrashing shark at the side of the boat is extremely dangerous. It's far better to use a flying gaff and the procedure outlined for roping off a big shark.

## ROPES

A tail rope may be made from 15 to 20 feet of ½-inch nylon rope with a loop at either end, or a loop on one end to secure to the fighting chair pedestal or a stern cleat and a stainless-steel snap at the other end, to loop back and snap to the line after being placed around the shark's tail.

A favorite tail rope of mine consists of 10 feet of $\frac{7}{16}$-inch stainless-steel cable encased in a like amount of yellow-braided nylon sleeve, connected to 8 feet of $\frac{7}{16}$-inch nylon line via a stainless-steel ring. At the terminal end of the section with the braided-nylon-sleeved stainless-steel cable is a heavy-duty stainless-steel snap, which, after the cable is wrapped around the shark's tail, is snapped to the standing part of the cable and drawn up tight. It's the finest style of tail rope I've ever used.

While on the subject of ropes, it's important to have a safety line available for each rod-and-reel outfit on board. A 6-foot-long piece of ¼-inch nylon rope is fine, with a loop on one end to attach to a rod holder, rail, or chair, and a stainless-steel snap at the other to attach to the reel's lugs. Often if a shark is hooked while the rod is in a rod holder, the pressure caused by the drag makes it difficult to remove the rod, and should you have it yanked from your hands, which does happen, the safety line will save losing the rod . . . and shark overboard.

I always use a safety line attached to the reel's lug when I'm in a fighting chair, which serves to keep people on board from being dragged from the chair while strapped to a bucket harness, and pos-

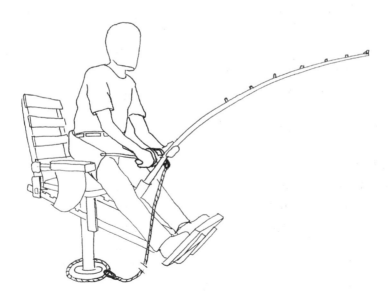

*When fighting really big sharks from a fighting chair, most anglers use a bucket harness, which they sit in. The harness is clamped to the reel, enabling the angler to use his legs to apply maximum pressure, sliding back and forth on the chair's seat as he gains line. Always use a safety line to secure the outfit to a rope collar around the stanchion of the fighting chair.*

sibly being dragged overboard. I also like to use a slightly longer safety line when I'm wearing a rod belt and shoulder harness and fighting a shark. With stand-up gear you're literally strapped in, and a slip or tumble while maneuvering along the rail could easily drag you overboard, especially with a strong shark, or should the reel's drag seize, as occasionally happens. The safety line's snap can be attached to a stern cleat, bow rail, or the fighting chair's pedestal while still giving you plenty of mobility.

Many anglers slip a rope doughnut over their fighting chair's pedestal and then use stainless-steel snaps at the end of their safety lines to snap onto the doughnut. The flying gaff rope can be snapped to the doughnut in much the same fashion.

## OTHER ESSENTIALS

### Filleting Table
It's a safe bet that you'll be using natural baits or chumming for sharks, and a filleting table makes handling natural baits and chunking chum less of a chore than having to kneel on the deck. My table measures 12 by 24 inches and is made of aluminum; it fits right into a gunwale-mounted rod holder. I cut a board to fit within the tray, which enables me to cut hook baits as desired, and to cut mackerel, butterfish, herring, and other baitfish as chunks for chum.

### Knives
Speaking of cutting reminds me how important it is to have some really sharp knives on board. If you have to cut chum chunks from a flat or two of menhaden, mackerel, or butterfish, a sharp knife is a godsend. I keep a pair of 8-inch-long filleting knives aboard for that purpose. I also have a pair of serrated knives of the same size, which are particularly effective when cutting through partially frozen baits.

### Buckets
A couple of 5-gallon buckets are a must, as frozen bunker, mackerel, and other baitfish usually come in cardboard flats, and once you

chunk the bait you'll need somewhere to put it. The 5-gallon plastic buckets are perfect, for you can then dispense the chum directly from them. The buckets are also useful when you want to make up a soupy chum composed of ground menhaden or mackerel and seawater.

## Chumming Accessories

I also keep a 5-gallon chum bucket on board that I fashioned for dispensing ground frozen chum. I used a drill saw of the kind used to cut a hole in a door for placement of a doorknob. I drilled a series of holes in the bottom and sides of the bucket, about a dozen in all. A frozen chum block is placed in the bucket, and the lid, which also has a couple of holes, is placed on securely. I then use an extra safety line to snap to the handle of the chum bucket and attach its loop to a stern cleat. The bucket is then eased overboard, where it hangs in the water. The rocking motion of the boat causes the thawing chum to ooze from the bucket, being carried away in a steady stream. I find this works better than delegating someone to the chumming chore, as it's the most effective way I've found of dispensing a steady, unbroken chum line.

Some anglers employ a mesh bag for this purpose, which I did when I began sharking years ago. I found it could present a problem when a hungry shark swam up and devoured the entire mesh bag, chum and all, in one fell swoop!

*A 5-gallon pail, with holes cut into it using a drill that cuts holes into doors where a doorknob is placed, is very effective for automatically dispersing chum. A block of frozen chum is placed in the bucket; the lid secured with rope and then hung off a stern cleat as you drift or slowly troll, permitting the chum to ooze from the bucket.*

It's also important to have a sizable ladle on board with a long handle, as well as a large, long-handled spoon such as those used in the kitchen while cooking. The ladle is the cleanest way to dispense a soupy chum, and the spoon is perfect for tossing out a spoonful of chunks as you drift along.

I also keep half a dozen hand towels in the cockpit, the kinds with a grommet in one corner and a shower curtain ring. One is hung on the fighting chair and another snapped to the filleting tray, as they're used many times during the day. Keep them wet; they'll clean your hands easier and won't get as smelly as a dry towel.

## Belts and Harnesses

The final pieces of equipment are those that are brought into play once a shark is hooked. If you have a big fighting chair on board, you'll need a bucket harness. The bucket harness is one in which you sit, with a seat portion and a back rounded to fit the curvature

*A fighting belt is important because it distributes the pressure from the rod butt and prevents injury. Using stand-up tackle and fighting a shark with a 30- or 50-pound-class outfit is comfortable even for handling big sharks, providing there is support with quick, maneuverable boat handling.*

of your back. Most have a fiberglass stiffener covered with channeled marine vinyl. Strong, adjustable straps with stainless-steel snaps extend from the harness.

Once a shark is hooked, you sit in the bucket harness and snap the harness to the reel's lugs. Rigged in this manner, you're able to periodically rest your arms. It's also important to have a safety line attached to the chair's pedestal and snapped to a strap on the bucket harness. This may seem overly cautious, but when fighting a big shark in a rough sea it's important that you not inadvertently be pulled from the chair while strapped into the bucket, rod, and reel, with a shark heading for the horizon.

For stand-up fishing you'll need a wide fighting belt with a gimbal, which protects your stomach from injury. Most have Velcro or pull-strap adjustments, which enable you to quickly slip one on and pull it tight. I caution you not to attempt to fight sharks without a fighting belt. I've done it on a couple of occasions and learned from the experience, having bruised my stomach and even my groin and thighs as I struggled to hold on while a big shark screamed line from the reel.

A shoulder or kidney harness used in conjunction with a fighting belt is the perfect combination. The shoulder harness fits much like a jacket, distributing the strain across your back with stainless-steel snaps attached to straps leading from the harness. With the snaps attached to the reel lugs and the butt of the rod in the fighting belt's gimbal, you're free to move about the boat with ease, and can periodically relax your arms to keep the muscles from tightening up during a protracted engagement with a big shark.

## Safety Line

By all means have a safety line attached for each outfit that is being fished, with a snap onto the harness lug of the reel and another snap to a rope doughnut around the fighting chair's pedestal. The twisted nylon safety lines should measure ⅜₆ inch in diameter and be 10 to 15 feet in length, enabling the anglers to move freely anywhere in the cockpit.

## Gloves and Pliers

As a shark is brought alongside, it usually becomes necessary for someone in the cockpit to handle the wire leader so the shark can be brought into range of a pair of pliers handled by another member of the crew. You should never attempt to handle a wire leader or stainless-steel cable leader without wearing a pair of heavy canvas gloves. Dry gloves prove unwieldy, so I always keep them in a bucket of water. Wear the gloves while wiring the shark; the person who is doing the gaffing should wear gloves as well, for you can rip up your hands quite easily if barehanded.

I've found Australian-made gloves, hand-cut and sewn, of treated water-resistant leather ideal. They're available in medium, large, and extra-large sizes, and extend well beyond your hand, offering maximum protection as you're wiring a big shark. I can't stress enough the importance of this critical piece of safety equipment.

An extremely strong pair of pliers is also important. I wear them in a sheath on my belt. It has a Velcro strap, which makes getting the pliers out of the sheath easy. The finest pliers I've ever used are the superstrong Sea Striker Billfishers, which will cut through tiny-diameter Spectra fishing line and 300-pound-test stainless-steel cable leader like a knife through butter.

Some sharkers also carry a pair of long-handled barbed-wire cutters. The handles are 18 to 30 inches in length and give you more added reach than conventional pliers. This enables you to keep your hands well away from the shark's jaw when cutting the wire or cable to release it.

## Anchors

Offshore you'll experience times when you may want to anchor so that your chum line drifts across underwater rocks, ledges, wrecks, or other structure where sharks seek forage.

A marker buoy with sufficient weighted line to reach bottom helps in marking a specific location once you've found it utilizing loran or GPS coordinates. Select a bright-colored buoy in hunter orange or hot pink, as these can readily be spotted from a distance in a rough sea.

To assist in pulling your anchor in deep-water situations, it's wise to have an anchor retrieval system on board. This system permits you to simply hook its stainless-steel ring, which is attached to a large buoy, around the anchor rope. The boat is then slowly throttled back in the direction of the anchor. As it comes taut, the buoy literally pulls the anchor free as the rope comes perpendicular to the bottom. As you continue to move forward, the rope slides through the retrieval ring until the anchor is pulled right to the surface and its chain slides

*Sharks frequently congregate around wrecks and broken, irregular bottom where there is an abundance of forage. It's always wise to carry 600 feet of anchor rope, a quality anchor, and a quick-release system with a ball buoy should you have to quickly leave the anchor to fight a shark. An anchor retrieval system makes for ease in recovering the anchor.*

into the ring. You then slowly back down toward the buoy, retrieving the line manually as you do so.

It's also good to have an automatic anchor release system on board, which leads from the anchor rope to the bridge. When a big shark is hooked, the engines are quickly started. With just a pull of a piece of ⅛-inch nylon cord, the anchor line—which is attached to a large marker buoy—is slipped from a cleated rope loop, with the buoy and anchor rope falling into the sea. The boat is then free to follow and land or release the shark, returning later to retrieve the buoy and anchor line using the anchor retrieval system. When anchored it's always wise to mark down the loran or GPS coordinates, so that you can easily return to the exact spot to locate and retrieve the buoy and anchor rope.

## Sea Anchor

Occasionally on the offshore shark grounds you'll experience strong winds that will result in the boat drifting faster than desirable. To slow the boat to an acceptable speed, a sea anchor is a great piece of equipment to have on board. A sea anchor is really a parachute, ranging in size from 9 feet in diameter for boats up to 25 feet, to 24 feet in diameter for boats from 40 to 90 feet.

The sea anchor is bridled with lines leading to the bow and stern in a moderate sea, or just from the bow in a heavy sea. It does a remarkable job of slowing the boat when strong wind conditions are encountered, and makes for a more comfortable drift. It also serves a purpose as a piece of safety equipment should you experience loss of power, stabilizing the movement of the boat and slowing its speed of drift.

## Other Gear

I like to keep a combination rigging and bait tray mounted in a rod holder on the out-of-the-way side of the boat across from where the lines are drifting. It's equipped with rigging needles, rigging twine, extra leaders and hooks, knives, and a cutting board. I can handle terminal rigging and baiting with ease while being out of the way of the activity on the other side of the boat should a strike be received.

While either drifting or anchored, some anglers employ an electronic device that emits acoustical tones that directly mimic the same pulsations made by swimming baitfish. Popularly called a Tuna Magnet, the device was originally designed to attract tuna to the boat while chumming, but is now available in a wide range of tones to attract not only tuna and marlin but specifically sharks as well.

The vibrations emitted by the electronic device can be heard at least a mile through the water, attracting sharks to investigate their source. The unit operates on 12-volt power and can be mounted with a through-hull mount in the bottom of the boat, or deployed directly over the side.

*Many shark fishermen have their boats equipped with an electronic device that emits sounds on a frequency that readily attracts sharks from a wide area.*

As I was researching this book I read of an Australian company that has created what it calls a Shark Shield, which does just the opposite of what the Tuna Magnet does: It emits electronic waves that interfere with a shark's sensory receptors, causing it to turn tail and swim away from the source. The Shark Shield is operated with batteries; attached to the ankle of swimmers, the 34-ounce unit is recommended to ward off shark attacks Down Under.

The scientific studies done as the Tuna Magnet and Shark Shield were developed bear out the sensitivity of sharks to sound. This knowledge, coupled with sharks' sensitivity to the variety of smells emitted by dead or dying fish, enable shark fishermen to capitalize on and exploit sharks' natural habits of seeking a food source.

These are the items of equipment that will make for enjoyable fishing while on the shark grounds. Some are more important than others, but you'll find that when the right gear is available it enables you to concentrate on the objective: finding and bringing a prized shark to boatside.

*The author at the helm of the Post 43 Linda June. It was equipped with a wide array of electronics that were helpful in locating sharks during two-day trips to waters of the northeast canyons and along the edge of the continental shelf.*

# 5

# Boats

Today's shark anglers are fortunate in that they have at their disposal a great selection of safe, seaworthy boats in which to head for the offshore grounds in search of their quarry. While many anglers choose to purchase their own boat, there are great shark fishing opportunities available while fishing from party boats, guide boats, and charter boats. Some guides along the coasts where sharks are plentiful specialize in this fishing, which accounts for the bulk of their clientele.

My first experience with sharks occurred aboard the party boat *Diana* with Captain Bob Ziegler at the helm. It sailed from Brielle, New Jersey, and on that eventful day we were targeting Atlantic mackerel during their spring sojourn north. On reaching the grounds the deckhands dispensed a soupy chum composed of ground menhaden diluted with seawater. The mackerel swarmed into the chum line and were most cooperative. In those days we used potato sacks tied to the rail, and by noon most of the bags had a comfortable bulge.

It was then that the skipper pointed out the fins of several sharks just off the bow. As a 16-year-old I was awestruck by the sight of the sleek sharks as they leisurely swam by, the first I'd ever seen. Then Captain Bob walked by and asked if I'd like to try my hand at catching one. You know the answer to that one.

He repaired to the pilothouse and returned with a shark rig, little more than a barrel swivel, 8 feet of stainless-steel leader wire, and an 8/0 O'Shaughnessy hook. After rigging up with one of the boat's sturdy party boat rods, with a 3/0 Penn Senator and 15-thread Cuttyhunk linen line, he grabbed a just-caught mackerel, walloped it on the rail to stun it, and placed the hook through its back. Handing me the outfit, he instructed me to let the stunned mackerel swim 40 to 50 feet from the boat.

With the reel in free spool and the clicker on, I held tight, not knowing what to expect. I didn't have to wait long, as a shark that had been swimming on the surface, its dorsal fin and tail breaking the surface suddenly, sank into the depths. Momentarily I felt a pickup, and the shark leisurely began to swim off with the mackerel, the reel's ratchet emitting its staccato as line left the reel.

"Lock up and hit 'em," instructed the good skipper. I did, and as I lifted back the shark realized something was amiss. It peeled line from the reel like a thing possessed.

Eventually the pressure I applied, helped along by the accompanying cheers of all on board, succeeded in getting the shark within range, and a huge gaff was planted in it and dragged across the rail. It was a blue shark as big as I was. The skipper cut the leader, tail-roped the shark, and with it still on the gaff, returned it over the rail, hanging from the rail where it couldn't do damage.

From that moment on I was a shark fisherman.

In those days the sharks caught aboard the packets were brought aboard and hung from a piling back at the dock, which drew a lot of onlookers, many of whom would sail the following day in the hope of a repeat performance. As long as the mackerel stayed in the area there was always a chance of catching the blue sharks, which followed the mackerel schools as they migrated.

After a stint in the Marine Corps during the Korean War, June and I married and vacationed in Florida, where I ran into Jack Robbins, an old Jersey friend and striper fanatic who'd retired to Florida and chartered his *Hawk* from Miami Beach.

It was then I experienced my first combat with a truly massive shark. We'd already released a sailfish and landed several big king mackerel when a huge brown shadow appeared under one of the skipping balao baits. Suddenly the shark's dorsal and tail broke the surface as it swam behind the bait. It followed for what seemed like an eternity, when suddenly the white water of the wake seemed to erupt as the huge shark, a hammerhead fully 8 feet in length, grabbed the balao.

What surprised me was that no one on board went for the rod, at which Jack laughingly said, "Go get 'em, Milt."

Go get 'em I did. I quickly learned why no one had gone for the rod, for the hammerhead was no blue shark. It was strong as an ox and made powerful, fast runs, often thrashing the surface wildly as it peeled line from the reel. Fortunately I was seated in a fighting chair with a footrest and buckled into a bucket harness, which gave me an opportunity to rest my arms; my forearms began to tighten up after the first half hour.

After much give-and-take and astute maneuvering of the boat, the mate got hold of the leader wire. While grasping the fine leader he applied pressure and deliberately broke it off. The hammerhead swam off, none the worse for its ordeal, and I sighed in relief!

It was but a year later that I had my first light-tackle shark encounter while fishing from a boat. It occurred while bonefishing out of Islamorada, in the Florida Keys. We were admittedly not able to even see a bonefish, let alone catch one. Then a 4-foot-long blacktip shark cruised within casting range, and the guide directed that I cast my live shrimp as close to its range of vision as I could.

I almost felt like a pro as the shrimp dropped in 3 feet ahead of the slowly cruising blacktip. Moments later the shark was thrashing across the thin water of the flats, the spinning reel screaming and the guide poling like crazy to keep up.

Miraculously the hook had embedded in the corner of the blacktip's jaw; otherwise its teeth would have gone through the 10-pound-test monofilament like a knife through butter. Everything held, and eventually the shark was alongside. A sharp yank by the guide on the delicate line freed the blacktip, and it leisurely swam away.

I site these three examples of a party boat, charter boat, and guide boat as being opportunities to catch sharks. Each instance proved to be a matter of an opportunity that presented itself, and in turn capitalizing on it. It's something that has happened frequently when fishing from the three different types of boats, ranging from the kelp beds of Ensenada, Mexico, to the Louisiana coast off South Pass and Bermuda's Challenger Banks, to name but a few.

*Many sharks frequent shallow tidal flats, especially in the Florida Keys and Bahamas. Here guide Andy Heild poles a shallow skiff as June Rosko fights a bonnethead shark at Walker's Cay in the Bahamas. Spinner sharks, blacktip sharks, and a variety of sandbar sharks frequent the shallows and provide exciting action on light tackle.*

*This bonnethead shark was caught by the author's wife, June, while fishing the flats at Walker's Cay in the Bahamas. A smaller member of the shark clan, the bonnethead is a determined adversary that is a challenge on light spinning tackle.*

With the passage of time, and quite honestly as we were able to afford one, we moved on to having the opportunity to fish from our own craft. I'd like to discuss and share with you some of the boats we've owned, and our likes and dislikes among the various types of craft that are available to the angler who takes his shark fishing seriously.

## THE THREE "LINDA JUNES"

After walking the aisles of several boat shows, and talking the talk with pitchmen, we spent many winter evening hours reviewing catalogs and specification sheets. Remember, we wanted a boat that could safely take us upward of 90 miles seaward. We wanted a comfortable boat, for during our travels we had fished on many boats that were less than desirable.

Indeed, we came to absolutely dislike fishing from the boats that are most often shown at boat shows. They're the center-console

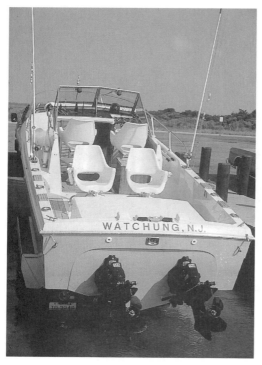

*The author's first* Linda June *was a 24-foot Wellcraft walkaround model with a pair of sponsons, where you could completely walk around the boat, wearing a fighting belt and kidney harness to fight a shark. When big sharks were hooked, anglers often sought the comfort of the two cockpit fighting chairs. The walkaround-style configuration is perfect for most shark fishing situations.*

models, on which you bake in the heat, freeze in the cold, are almost certain to get soaked in the slightest chop. Most don't have a head, which rules them out as a family boat. Nor do they have bunks; nor is there adequate storage. They have absolutely no redeeming social values, nor are they a good boat for shark fishing.

Ultimately we decided on what at the time was the first walkaround cuddy cabin boat. It was a Wellcraft with an Airslot hull featuring a pair of sponsons, which made the boat look like an ugly duckling. Still, it was the most stable boat of its size I've ever fished from.

Our first *Linda June* was named for our daughter, Linda, and my wife, June. It was 24-footer, with an 8-foot beam, and sported a pair of 140-horsepower Mercruiser stern drives, which gave us a top-end speed of 25-plus knots. The below-sole fuel tank carried a full 100 gallons of gasoline, which gave us great range. Its cuddy cabin came complete with head. It could sleep three, had ample storage, and had a Bimini top and enclosure for inclement weather.

Importantly, it could be trailered on an E-Z Loader trailer, which we hitched to a Chevy Suburban to fish from Florida to New England, wherever game fish and sharks could be found.

On board we had all the Coast Guard safety-mandated equipment, such as life jackets, safety flares, whistle, and running lights, along with a first-aid kit.

At first we had a radio direction finder that we used in conjunction with a compass for navigation. Eventually we moved up to loran, which was a godsend for pinpointing shark fishing grounds, such as offshore lumps and ridges, and the various offshore canyons. A VHF radio was added for communication.

We further equipped the boat as a mini sportfisherman, complete with a pair of helm seats and a pair of small fighting chairs, along with seven gunwale-mounted rod holders. Two rail-mounted rod holders were placed on the bow rail. On each side of the cuddy cabin there were a pair of vertical rod holders that could accommodate all the outfits on board, so there was a spot to put them out of the way while fighting a fish. A pair of outriggers were also added.

For purposes of just shark fishing, this was the best boat we'd ever had or fished from. The reason was simply its walkaround feature, which enabled you to easily and safely walk completely around the boat while fighting a shark. This, by the way, is the norm, as most sharks rip up the ocean and at one time or another go in every conceivable direction.

My son-in-law, Joe Basilio, and daughter-in-law, Kelly Rosko, both caught their first sharks aboard this boat while fishing the beautiful waters off Block Island, Rhode Island. I vividly recall a day with Kelly fighting a big blue shark while seated in the fighting chair, while Joe had to work his way to the bow with a brute of a blue shark. Each shark was going in a different direction, yet we didn't even have to start the engines, as Joe could easily reach the bow thanks to the walkaround feature. Kelly's was the first to be released, after which Joe took the chair and eventually released one that was bigger than he is!

Attempting to do this on bigger boats that we've owned was a task, to put it mildly, and to put it more properly, very unsafe. This is especially true when you're harnessed to a big shark and attempting to climb from the cockpit to the forward deck, and then maneuvering along railings that are designed to be aesthetic, not safe. Some boats, for the sake of ego, don't even come with bow rails, which is ridiculous. One slip, or a reel freezing up, and you could wind up in the water in a split second—all the while with a rod belt and shoulder harness attached to a heavy rod and reel, amd a big shark on the other end.

The irony is that this boat had the perfect hull, and the perfect cabin and cockpit configuration, and was soon discontinued by the manufacturer! The reason: It looked like an ugly duckling, with its

winglike sponsons on each side of the hull turning off the buying public. The net result was that aesthetics of a semi-V hull design won out over the stability of the sea-keeping qualities of the deep-V design with its pair of sponsons. It was a real shame.

Of course the first *Linda June* didn't have the creature comforts a bigger boat could offer, so after seven years of superb service, and the engines growing weary, we decided to move up.

Our choice was a 33-foot Bertram convertible powered with a pair of 3208T Caterpillar diesel engines and a generator, which would make overnight trips

*The author's second* Linda June *was a 33-foot diesel-powered Bertram that was an excellent seaworthy craft capable of extended trips to offshore canyons. Sharks are nocturnal in their feeding habits, and often while chumming tuna in canyon waters huge sharks would be attracted to the chum. A quick switch to wire or cable leaders often resulted in fast action under the quartz lights 100 or more miles from shore.*

possible. It comfortably slept four and had a convertible dinette, refrigerator, huge freshwater tank, heat and air-conditioning, stand-up head and shower, and loads of storage and closets.

Importantly, its fuel capacity gave us ample range to reach the offshore canyons with ease while at an economical 25-knot cruise speed.

The boat had an aluminum tuna tower, which gave us excellent vantage, especially when searching for sharks finning on the surface. We had a Rybovich fighting chair with footrest installed in the cockpit, six flush-mounted rod holders, a pair of outriggers, and quartz lights. We were ready for the sharks, tuna, and billfish of the deep.

The array of electronics on the bridge included radar, VHF radio, loran, and a paper chart recorder that was a godsend at the time. The recorder enabled us to observe not only the bottom conformation but also schools of fish and, yes, even individual sharks and tuna as they cruised beneath the hull!

The boat was admittedly a big step up in comfort, especially while living aboard for extended two-day trips to the canyons. Importantly, it was big enough that we didn't take a beating returning home when seas had built to a height we hadn't anticipated. It felt good having a solid Bertram hull under us. The shortcoming was that all the fishing had to be done from the cockpit, and whenever a double hookup was experienced it presented a dilemma, unless either fish or sharks stayed aft, often requiring delicate maneuvering in order to prevent losing one of the fish.

We fished the Bertram 33 for five years, and then got that urge to move on, for with a bigger boat we could expand our angling horizons, not just to the north and south, but easterly as well.

Our biggest *Linda June* was a Post 43, and ideally suited for extended stays of two or three days offshore. Falling into the category of convertible sportfisherman, it more properly might be termed a floating home, for it had every amenity you could expect.

Twin 671TI Detroit Diesel engines powered the Post 43, each developing 500 horsepower, which moved the dreadnought along at

*The author's Post 43, the third* Linda June, *was ideal for offshore excursions to the canyons and continental shelf for periods of several days' duration. Carrying more than 500 gallons of diesel fuel, it had the capability of heading for shelf waters where few shark fishermen ventured.*

a respectable 30 knots. The boat weighed 33,000 pounds and carried 500 gallons of diesel fuel plus 100 gallons of fresh water. A generator provided electric power, which is so important on overnighters.

Air-conditioning and heating made for comfortable temperatures while sleeping on board. The creature comforts accommodated six, in two staterooms and a convertible couch in the salon. A beautiful head, complete with stall shower, was a comfort after a day or two on the water. The galley had running water and an electric range and oven. A microwave was also included. A full-sized stand-up refrigerator-freezer held ample food and beverages for an extended offshore sharking excursion.

A pair of color television sets and omnidirectional TV antenna enabled us to pick up good signals from up to 100 miles from shore. The television in the salon had the biggest screen, and we had the electronic fishfinder tied in to it. This enabled us to fish in the cockpit while observing the screen through the window in the door leading to the salon. The size of the screen, coupled with the brilliant colors, enabled us to see schools of baitfish, medium-sized fish, and huge individual sharks and tuna as they cruised beneath the transducer. It was a perfect setup for anyone owning a boat with a television set to pursue, as the cost was nominal and the advantages tremendous, far superior than trying to monitor the small screens of most fishfinders.

The bridge electronics included radar, a pair of VHF radios, autopilot, a pair of fishfinders, a single sideband radio with worldwide capability, loran, and a loud hailer with communications to the salon. We also had quartz lights that illuminated the cockpit to near daytime brightness, a foghorn, and both fixed and portable searchlights.

The cockpit was rigged for fishing, with an International big-game fighting chair, complete with footrest and four rod holders. There were also six gunwale-mounted rod holders. A series of easily accessible gaffs, ranging from hand gaffs to long-handled single gaffs, tagging stick, line pusher, and flying gaffs and ropes were stored in racks beneath the covering boards. A sink, rigging table, cabinets, and saltwater washdown hose were conveniently located. The transom had a door for bringing big fish aboard that we used for broadbill swordfish and tuna, but not sharks, which we never brought aboard for safety reasons.

The spacious cockpit of the Post 43 made it ideally suited to big-game fishing. For fighting big tuna, billfish, and sharks, the International fighting chair proved ideal, especially when using 50- and 80-pound-class tackle, which for many is far too heavy and cumbersome to use while standing up. For anglers desiring to go toe-to-toe with tuna and sharks while wearing a shoulder harness and fighting belt, and using 30- or 50-pound-class tackle, there was cockpit coaming padding all around, which cushioned the thighs from bruising while fighting fish.

Overall, the big boat was the way to go when making far-offshore treks in search of big sharks, billfish, and tuna along the edge of the continental shelf. For in those far-offshore waters, which are where the heavyweights are often found, the weather can be beautiful with an ocean as flat as a millpond. It can all change very quickly, however, and suddenly you're confronted with winds of 20-plus knots and seas that can get awesome. There's a great comfort level in heading for home with ample fuel on board and a hull beneath you that can take all the pounding the ocean has to offer.

I recall one particularly rough day, with awesome seas, where we came off a head sea. For a moment the entire boat literally was airborne, then crashed into an incoming sea while cruising at 25 knots. The shock broke one of the four steel engine mounts and sheared three of the four steel bolts holding the generator in place. It ripped the omnidirectional television antenna from the top of the bridge enclosure, which is now at the bottom of the sea. Fortunately we just plodded along, fighting the seas for several more hours to cover the remaining 85 miles to the inlet. Earlier that morning we were trolling shortly after daybreak in what was perhaps a 2-foot chop!

Our three *Linda June*s represent the broad spectrum of small, medium, and large boats that are ideally suited to seeking sharks in offshore waters. The Wellcraft 24 Airslot walkaround was by far the most fun to fish from, providing the weather was nice, and was ideal for quick one-day junkets. The Bertram 33 filled the midrange and could well be termed the happy medium with respect to size, range, equipment, and creature comforts. The Post 43 was a fishing machine that's hard to beat. Bottom line, it comes down to personal choice.

## SELECTING A SHARK BOAT

Today the nice part of selecting a boat is that the majority of builders are turning out quality products. The nature of the business is such that competition, seaworthiness and design of the product, plus safety considerations, have caused many builders to fall by the wayside, which benefits the boating public.

Each year sees innovations in boat design, all to the betterment of those who head down to the sea to hunt sharks. State-of-the-art electronics keep improving each year, with miniaturization and

*For maximum efficiency on the offshore shark grounds, boatmen employ the latest electronics, including a water temperature gauge, color scope for locating forage, and loran or Global Positioning System for locating underwater canyons and other structure.*

combining units such as radar, fishfinders, and plotters all making for a comfortable, uncluttered helm and great reliability. Global positioning systems are gradually replacing loran. The GPS units can be programmed to take you 100 miles to sea and position you directly above your favorite shark wreck. Computers enable you have a variety of data at your fingertips, from long-range weather forecasts to immediate weather updates, sea temperature charts, and other information that expands your horizon and enables you to better enjoy the sport.

One piece of equipment you most certainly should include aboard is an inflatable life raft. Over the years I've known of several capable seamen aboard excellent, top-quality craft who encountered difficulty that was totally unexpected. Had it not been for the inflatable life raft, fatalities could have resulted.

In addition to the three basic boats that we've owned over a span of more than 25 years, the changes haven't been that drastic when it comes to hull design. The deep-V and modified-V hulls, complete with variations that builders incorporate into their designs, are pretty much the norm.

An exception was the Wellcraft Airslot with its ugly-duckling sponsons. Another design that has greatly impressed me as a great all-around seaworthy hull, with all the characteristics I like in a shark boat, is the catamaran hull. In the past five years the cats have taken the seacoast by storm, particularly boats in the 24- to 32-foot range.

The catamarans of this size are awesome boats. They do fall into the ugly-duckling category, which turns off a lot of people; they don't have the pleasant lines of a conventional hull. But putting appearance aside—and many of the cats' appearance features have improved over the last couple of years—the boats have excellent sea qualities, are roomy, and feature cockpit designs and walkaround features that make them perfect for shark fishing. Admittedly, they don't have the elaborate creature comforts of many of the big boats, but they certainly warrant your attention when in the market for a reliable shark boat.

The catamarans have a number of power options, including a pair of four-cycle outboards that are extremely reliable and fuel-efficient. Some cats also have inboard diesels with stern drive units—a superb power combination that gives you reliability, range, very economical fuel consumption, and minimal maintenance.

Make no mistake: Purchasing a boat for offshore shark fishing adventures is not to be taken lightly. I spent many hours walking the aisles of boat shows, looking in engine rooms and evaluating power plants and equipment, and especially electronics, before making a decision on what to purchase. I can say the time was well spent, for I was never disappointed, and all three boats lived up to my expectations.

Once you narrow down your choices, and there are many, and decide on the "perfect" boat for your area and needs, don't hesitate to call an on-the-water dealer, or even the builder, and take a test ride. There's nothing better than getting on the water aboard the boat you plan to buy. Bring your wife and the children along too, as the boat invariably becomes a family thing, and their input will

*The author's first* Linda June *was trailerable, which enabled the Rosko clan to fish from New England to the Florida Keys with ease. The hull was designed with a pair of sponsons, which gave the craft excellent stability, minimal pounding in a heavy sea, and fine sea-keeping qualities in almost any sea condition.*

prove invaluable. When everybody's happy it's the beginning of many years of enjoyment. Don't hesitate to ask questions, questions, and more questions. Poke around every nook and cranny on the boat, so that when you make the final decision you're set in your mind that this is the boat for you.

A final word of caution is in order, and I cannot emphasize it enough. Shark fishing far offshore can be very rewarding and enjoyable. Never forget, however, that sea conditions can, and often do, change in less time than it takes me to write this sentence. Safety should always be of paramount concern. Check several different weather reports before heading to the offshore grounds. Use common sense in evaluating whether or not you should head for the shark grounds. If the weather is questionable, by all means cancel the trip. There will be many other opportunities when the weather is nice and conditions are conducive to enjoyable fishing.

It's ironic, as I conclude this chapter, that a disastrous event took place just this past weekend. A shark fishing tournament based in Long Island continued as scheduled, in defiance of a horrendous weather forecast. The decision to sail, of course, is always at the option of the captain. On this particular day more than 10 boats left the inlet, and all encountered enormous 8- to 10-foot-high waves and extremely strong wind. Most were quick to turn and head back to port.

Unfortunately a 24-foot boat, with four anglers aboard, encountered weather they simply could not handle. Their frantic distress calls via VHF radio and cell phone calls to 911 were received, but to no avail; search parties were unable to find the boat or its occupants. Today's news, as I write this, was that one body was found floating yesterday off the Jersey coast.

Boats are a big investment. The time you spend before your purchase is time well spent and will lay the groundwork for years of fun on blue water. Just never forget that safety must be your paramount concern as you head to sea for the offshore grounds. And use common sense when fishing for sharks—they too can present dangers if handled carelessly.

# 6

# Finding
# Sharks

It may sound like an oversimplification, but wherever there's a plentiful supply of forage you're apt to find sharks, whether it be in the protected reaches of coastal bays or on the broad expanse of ocean, hundreds of miles from shore.

Inshore sharks are more easily found, simply because the grounds they frequent are more confining and readily accessible. Classic examples are the blacktip sharks that frequent the flats of the Florida Keys, the leopard sharks that cruise among the kelp beds off the southern California coast, or the sandbar sharks that move into New Jersey and Delmarva bays during the summer months.

Locating the offshore sharks and pelagic species that travel the waters of the world offers a greater challenge. Some travel alone, while others forage in small groups. Many travel thousands of miles in the course of a season, their movements dictated by a variety of factors, including water temperature, but most important is the availability of food.

The author's son, Bob, sets out a kite line from which are suspended a pair of outrigger clips; into these are snapped two rigged lines, each with a live bait positioned to swim just beneath the surface. When a shark strikes, the line is released from the clip, and as soon as the line comes taut the action begins!

When I began shark fishing the only information about the availability of sharks was passed down by word of mouth. Commercial fishermen who worked the offshore grounds with their draggers would herald the arrival of the first blue sharks, hard on the tails of the migrating mackerel. Scallop draggers working off the Virginia capes would herald the arrival of mako sharks that moved up to feed on the discards and trash the crew shoveled overboard.

Bits of information such as this, accumulated over a period of years, enabled early shark fishermen to prepare a matrix of the areas that were apt to provide good action. This historical data, coupled with the use of geodetic survey charts of offshore grounds, worked remarkably well.

Keep in mind that the shark populations on the Atlantic, Pacific, and Gulf coasts 50 years ago were what you might call normal; they hadn't been depleted by either commercial or sportfishing interests. It was easier to locate sharks simply because there were more of them.

Indeed, during that era many thoughts of sharks as a pest, and it was a common practice to just kill them for no apparent reason other than their being dangerous to handle. I vividly recall fishing aboard a party boat out of Biloxi, Mississippi, where the captain each day would catch a little tunny (called bonito locally) and place it on a huge shark hook with a chain leader. The shark rig was then tied to a piece of ½-inch anchor line, baited up with the tunny, and unceremoniously flung overboard. Eventually a several-hundred-pound bull shark would take the bait and thrash about for hours, then be hauled alongside and tied from a block and tackle when it was time to return to port. The shark would be displayed for the tourists visiting the docks each day, and the carcass transported back to sea and dumped the following day. This was repeated almost daily, killing thousands of mature sharks in the process.

Then came the shark tournaments, where along the Long Island and New Jersey coasts there was a mass carnage of blue, mako, thresher, and tiger sharks. Literally hundreds of sharks were brought to the docks. Many were too small to even bother weighing, and they were tied off to a stern cleat, towed back out the inlet, and dumped. Many washed up on bathing beaches. Looking back, the whole tournament scene of that era was disgusting—and the tournaments still go on.

As you'll see as you continue reading this book, I am not a fan of fishing tournaments of any kind, which I feel turn a contemplative pastime into a competitive sport. While the public doesn't often realize it, tournaments are a moneymaking business, and the promoters go to great lengths to provide the biggest purses, greatest prizes, and most hoopla to generate the biggest number of boats. They also go to great lengths to catch and kill lots of fish, and contributed greatly during the 1970s and '80s to the demise of many species of sharks. In fairness, however, it must be said that tournaments have been a source of scientific information and samples.

Indeed, just within the past few days I've read of several tournaments boasting of the great catches of mako sharks that had been weighed. From the scientific knowledge available to me, not one of these sharks had grown large enough to reproduce!

I make mention of this indiscriminate slaughter of the shark population to show how a resource can virtually be destroyed. Indeed, in recent years there have been shark tournaments held in which not a single shark is caught, simply because the population has been so severely depleted. While commercial fishermen have done their share of harm to mako and other marketable sharks, and can be condemned for the practice of cutting off shark fins for the market and then releasing the disabled sharks, the sportfishing community must bear some of the burden of responsibility for what's happened to the shark populations over the last three decades.

While there are unquestionably fewer offshore sharks available today, the anglers who seek them have a variety of tools at their disposal that better enable them to concentrate their efforts in waters where sharks are most apt to be located.

## WATER TEMPERATURE

Perhaps the most important of all the technically advanced tools now available to the offshore angler are satellite charts of surface

water temperatures. Among these are Offshore Satellite Services
temperature charts for canyon fishermen seeking tuna and marlin.
My good friend Captain Len Belcaro originally began providing
these. As it turns out, these charts are an extremely useful tool for
the shark fisherman, but for a somewhat different reason. With tuna
and marlin the charts are most often used to identify temperature
breaks, where ideal ranges where the fish generally congregate are
72 degrees or higher. Many sharks, especially the mako, prefer temperature ranges from 58 to 68 degrees. Hence the charts prove useful in that shark trollers or chummers can avoid the warm side of
the temperature break, concentrating their efforts where the water
temperature is cooler and more to the sharks' liking.

What is especially significant in using temperature charts is that
they clearly define where temperature breaks occur, especially where

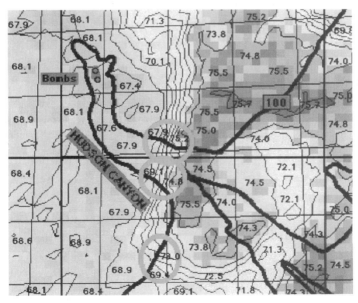

Len Belcaro's Offshore Satellite Service charts clearly show the water
temperatures of the offshore canyons where sharks congregate. This
sample shows the great range of water temperatures, which delineates
just where the forage species, plus tuna and marlin, are found—which
is where sharks are also apt to be feeding.

a warm core eddy injects itself into surrounding cooler water, often extending for a great distance into it. This break, where there is a significant gradient, is invariably where the forage congregates. Recognize that sharks are opportunists, and not averse to feeding on a wide variety of forage. I've removed many small fish, on up to huge chunks of tuna, from the stomach of sharks. It's at the temperature breaks that the small forage—the mackerel, bonito, jacks, sardines, and other fish—congregates, in turn attracting the marlin and tuna. The sharks too are close at hand, although many will avoid the warmest side of the break.

As I'll often note throughout this book, some of the finest shark fishing is experienced at night. I suspect it's because during the day many shark species will avoid the warm surface water, retreating into the depths. As the sun sets and the surface water cools, lots of the forage species will also move toward the surface film, and the sharks are not far behind.

It's especially significant to note that while fishing far-offshore waters during the day, you'll seldom observe sharks sunning themselves on the surface when the weather is extremely warm. The sharks are there, but in the depths. With cloud cover, or an influx of cooler water, suddenly the sharks' presence becomes apparent.

While fishing the Hudson Canyon off New Jersey I've often trolled for several days without spotting a shark on the surface. However, just prior to the fall migration of tuna and marlin, as the water temperatures drop to less than 70 degrees, I've observed dozens of sharks, including makos, hammerheads, threshers, and tigers, on the surface. It was almost like cruising through an aquarium.

I vividly recall one hectic late-autumn day's trolling for yellowfin and bigeye tuna and long-finned albacore. Sharks were apparent in the area, although we did not target them. It was a day we returned to dockside early, as we had all the tuna that our crew could possibly use for freezing and canning for the upcoming winter.

Just two days later we made another trip to the same area of the Hudson, and while heading offshore heard the single-sideband radio chatter of party boat skippers who were returning from their overnight trips. Among the several boats on the frequency we heard reports of not a single fish. It was as if there wasn't a fish in the ocean. Undeterred, we sailed on. Upon arriving at the loran coordinates where we'd been successful earlier, we found not a trace of life

There were no porpoises, no sharks, no readings of bait or tuna, nor any bird life. As I had observed several years earlier, the mass migration of tuna had occurred in just a single day, and everything else went with the tuna, including the sharks. It was a phenomenon you've got to experience to appreciate. When the time came to move on, it must have been that Mother Nature fired a starter's pistol, and the entire canyon family vacated their summer quarters!

Bluefin tuna generally prefer cooler water than yellowfin tuna or albacore, and their migration north brings them closer to shore. The school bluefin is a tasty treat to mako and blue sharks, and these prized sharks often follow the inshore route along the 30- to 40-fathom line.

Where Len's Offshore Satellite Service charts, and those of other satellite providers, prove most helpful is in saving you countless hours of cruise time trying to find the location of a warm core eddy. Once you locate the eddy and its accompanying temperature break, you can develop a strategy as to how to fish the area.

I always make it a point to take a few minutes to cruise through an area where I've encountered the temperature breaks of the warm core eddy. I watch the fishfinder for signs of bait and tuna on which sharks feed, and observe the direction of the current on a windless day, or the wind direction if its speed will impact the drift.

Then I set up my drift, ideally to move along the edge of the break line, which is possible with a light current and no wind. If it's howling you've just got to give it your best shot, setting up ½ mile or so from where you feel the break exist, and either working from the warm side to the cooler side, or vice versa. Here it's important to watch your sea temperature gauge and monitor your fishfinder, quickly noting your loran or GPS coordinates once a strike is received. In this way, as you drift away from the ideal combination to fight or land a shark, you'll have a set of numbers that you can return to. You can also search out comparable water temperatures to capitalize on the fact that you hooked sharks in what apparently was a temperature they preferred.

## MAPPING TECHNOLOGY

The effectiveness of using satellite water temperature charts can be enhanced considerably by combining it with computer technology. Maptech, a Massachusetts company, is a leader in digital mapping, with software that includes more than 60,000 charts and maps. I've used the Maptech charts and they're almost beyond belief, giving a complete picture of the seafloor.

A unique feature is that the software gives you a three-dimensional view of the underwater landscape, enhanced with a new contour dead-ahead feature. The software permits you to tilt, spin, and view the underwater world from any angle. While it takes a while to get used to, once you get the hang of it you become immersed in bringing together the relationship of warm core eddies, surface water temperatures, and the configuration of the bottom where these factors come together.

I've found Maptech's three-dimensional contour charts unique in that they don't require having a computer on board, which was essential with most earlier charting systems. You can download their Pocket Contour to a handheld computer and you're all set to sail to the offshore grounds.

The unique features of this system include 3-D charts, software, and a shipwreck/obstruction database. The display grid uses 50-meter offshore resolution and 10-meter inshore resolution. Importantly, it permits you to follow the canyons and bottom structure with ease. This is what determines where the forage will congregate, and the game fish and sharks in turn are attracted to where an easy meal is in the offing.

The software has a spin, tilt, and zoom feature to three-dimensionally view the bottom where wrecks, rocks, ridges, or lumps are located. You can then switch to your fishfinder and often observe schools of forage such as squid and butterfish. Sometimes you'll

*Bull sharks are a formidable adversary that will test an angler's tackle and skill to the limit. They have a wide range and, typical of most sharks, readily respond to a bait drifted in a chum line, or will crash a slow-trolled natural bait.*

observe schools of tuna in close proximity to the forage. It is not at all unusual to pinpoint the profile of sharks as they cruise along, particularly if you've a high-end fishfinder.

A recently introduced feature of Maptech's Offshore Navigator software is its Spherical-Horizon View. This gives you an image as though you'd draped a NOAA paper chart over a beach ball. Up close and far away are both depicted in one dramatic chart, where you see your immediate area in clear detail but also see where you are heading. As you move across the water, the Spherical-Horizon View advances and the chart automatically refocuses to keep everything in perspective.

The bottom configuration is important, as offshore lumps, rocks, ledges, and canyons all hold a multitude of forage. While newcomers often think of sharks as traveling in the upper strata of the water column, many sharks, especially tiger sharks, are deep feeders, often scouring the bottom as they search for a meal. Thus, by being aware of just what the bottom looks like, you can enhance your opportunities by positioning your boat and lines to fish some baits very deep, and others at different depths in the water column. Veteran shark anglers, especially veteran charter boatmen who specialize in shark fishing, often log every shark they catch, including the depth at which it was hooked, location, water temperature, and any pertinent data on concentrations of forage or other sea life in the area.

Over a period of time a pattern develops, with tiger sharks hooked on deep-set bait and makos and threshers on baits near the surface, where it's often possible to almost hand-feed them.

## SECRETS OF THE GREAT SHARK CAPTAINS

Captain Bill Verbanas★, who sailed his charter boat *Reelistic* from Delaware, enjoyed remarkable success with truly big sharks. His anglers landed mako sharks up to 942 pounds. They've also scored with many other species, primarily thresher, porbeagle, blue, and tiger sharks.

Bill was not content to fish the inshore waters, which is where most of the shark anglers along the middle Atlantic coast concentrate their efforts. His success came about through prodding far-offshore waters. To many shark fishermen this means sailing 50 or 75 miles seaward. Not so with Bill, as he set his sights on the sharks, tuna, dolphin, and marlin that set up residence in waters beyond the edge of the continental shelf. It was not at all uncommon for him to sail more than 100 miles offshore.

His pioneering spirit discovered an almost magical difference between fishing the waters beyond the edge, where the depth drops from 200 or 300 fathoms to 1,500 fathoms or more. While sailing from most middle and north Atlantic coastal ports this meant a trip of 100 to 120 miles or more before the fishing grounds are reached.

---

★Billy Verbanas, the extremely talented skipper of the Delaware-based REEL-ISTIC was wiring a particularly aggressive mako shark estimated to weigh 400 pounds on July 9, 2002. He took a wrap on the wire in an attempt to pull it within range for gaffing. In a last minute lunge the big shark pulled Bill from the boat and he disappeared beneath the waves. When he surfaced the crew reached him and attempted to resuscitate him, to no avail, as he had drowned. Note additional information on page vi, In Memoriam. The author had communicated with Billy Verbanas just weeks prior to this tragedy while writing this book.

Coupled with his preference for fishing these far-offshore waters, he sought spots where the surge of a warm eddy clashes with the colder water, as it is in this confluence that huge schools of baitfish congregate. This in turn attracts a wide variety of game fish such as bigeye tuna, yellowfin tuna, albacore, dolphin, wahoo, white marlin, blue marlin, and even sailfish on occasion. This setting of huge schools of forage species, plus concentrations of squid beyond belief, results in a situation where big sharks congregate to enjoy.

*The author fights a tough mako shark he hooked while fishing a bluefish fillet bait as they were anchored and seeking bluefish. It always pays to put out a shark rig when seeking other species on which sharks feed, as it often results in a bonus catch.*

This phenomenon of really big sharks staying in the far-offshore waters while their smaller brethren move inshore to what are commonly referred to as shelf waters is something that causes even scientists to ponder. But the pattern persists, and if you stay inshore of the 1,500-fathom line you'll consistently catch smaller sharks than when you venture out into the deep.

However, just going into the deep isn't necessarily a key to success. You won't be as concerned about bottom configuration, which is of little consequence when you're in 1,500 fathoms. The key is observing surface water temperature, looking for signs of life. Bird life usually indicates that fish have been or are feeding in an area, for the birds are picking up the scraps left by tuna and sharks. Whales and porpoises are also a good sign, for they require a great deal of forage. Because they must regularly surface for air, their presence is readily apparent.

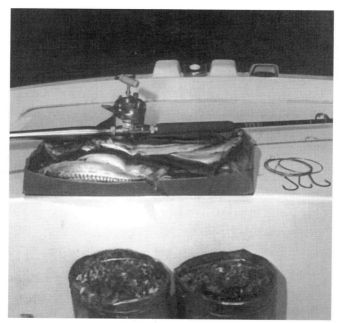

*Night fishing will often result in more action from sharks than fishing during the day. All you'll require are a couple of cans of ground chum, a flat of baitfish, several hooks rigged on wire leaders, and a quality 30-pound-class stand-up outfit. Many sharks take up residence within 20 miles of shore and are well within range of small-boat anglers.*

In the deep, much as on shelf waters, the sharks often seek cooler water during the day. The same is true of forage species and game fish such as tuna. Toward dusk the forage moves toward the surface, and the sharks do the same, resulting in a greater degree of activity near the surface than is usually experienced during hours of daylight.

The drawback of fishing in the 1,500-fathom depths beyond the continental shelf is the time it takes to get there. You're talking about many hours of travel time to cover 100 to 125 miles seaward. The trip, even with a fast boat, is best scheduled as a two-day event, sailing offshore in hours of daylight, then setting up for an afternoon and night bite. While the fishing is often torrid during hours of darkness, the bite gets particularly hot during what is often called first light—that hour or so before there's really much visibility. I suspect the game fish and sharks realize daybreak is nearing and they'll soon be moving into the depths, so they fill their stomachs with reckless abandon, providing shark anglers with a hectic bite.

Trips beyond the continental shelf are best done with big boats, for even the best-made plans and weather monitoring don't ensure that you'll have calm seas for the duration of the trip. You want to make certain to have a sound hull under you that can take the punishment of a long return trip should the weather turn nasty.

As a result of the time frame required to travel these great distances, many of the veteran anglers who specialize in far-offshore trips make them of two or three days' duration. Anglers and crew sleep in shifts, as it's just too physically exhausting to stay awake. Trips of this magnitude take a great deal of planning, from topping off fuel tanks to having on board ample engine oil, chum, bait, food,

*This mako shark was hooked on a bluefish fillet as anglers chummed for bluefish.*
*All sharks frequent areas where bottom fish and game fish are plentiful, as they're able*
*to obtain a meal with ease.*

and beverages. Should this type of adventure interest you, I'd suggest an exploratory trip with a seasoned professional like Bill Verbanas, so that you get the feel of what's entailed should you elect to go it alone on a future trip, and be in a position to capitalize on your experience.

Anglers who target the salmon sharks in Alaska do not have the luxury of being able to head such great distances offshore, as the waters of the Gulf of Alaska are often treacherous. They experience a substantial tidal range, which causes a churning action of the water without the pronounced temperature breaks experienced elsewhere. Charter skippers who ply Alaska's waters, such as Captain Andy Mezirow, depend on structure to find their sharks. Fortunately, the bottom structure is such is that skippers can employ their electronics to visit haunts where they've previously scored. Most of the relatively small number of shark fishing professionals in Alaska keep detailed accounts of such structure where they've previously caught sharks and regularly return to these known haunts. For structure draws the sharks much like a magnet; they know from earlier visits that there's plenty of forage available—in this case often salmon—to satisfy their appetites.

Knowing the migration patterns of sharks helps in determining where you should fish. Captains like Andy Dangelo, who skippers his *Maridee II* out of Galilee, Rhode Island, can predict quite accurately when sharks will arrive in his area. He watches the surface water temperature, and when it reaches 57 degrees he knows the blue sharks will be there. Once it jumps beyond 60 degrees the prize makos will arrive.

He maintains detailed logs of his catches and knows that bottom structure is the key to his scoring with the variety of sharks that visit Little Rhody's waters. He likes structure and wrecks in particular, because that's where herring and mackerel populate the mid-depths of the water column. The wrecks in particular have an abundance of ling, sea bass, and tautog during the summer months. While hugging the bottom, these species regularly afford an easy-to-obtain meal for sharks.

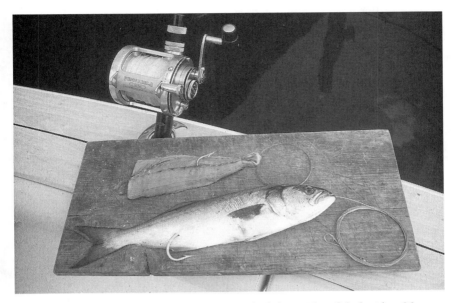

*A whole bluefish, or a fillet of bluefish, is a fine shark bait. When fished with a 30- or 50-pound-class stand-up outfit, the angler enjoys maximum sport. Sharks are found wherever there is an abundance of forage, be it tuna in the northeast canyons, snappers and groupers on the southern reefs, or around the kelp beds of the Pacific.*

When he reaches his favorite offshore haunts, Andy will take into account the wind direction and drift, and set up so the breeze will carry him over or just near his favorite structure. He favors a 10- to 15-mile-per-hour breeze, which briskly moves the boat along and enables him to cover a lot of bottom. He has a live well in the hull of his charter rig and places a frozen block of ground chum in it; as the boat drifts along, the chum thaws and oozes from the live well. The advantage of his system is that the chum is always working, and you never have a break in the chum line. Andy also uses a liberal amount of fish oil to supplement the ground chum and finds that it excites the sharks, which pick up the scent of the oil but can't zero in on the fish they think it's coming from. Once they get the scent of the hook bait, they're onto it in a flash.

Also a believer in watching water temperatures to indicate the arrival of sharks is thresher shark fishing specialist Captain Chet

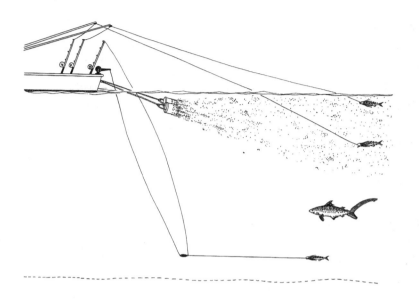

*A plastic 5-gallon bucket or two, with holes cut into it, can be tied off and used while trolling or chumming, as it permits a steady stream of thawing ground chum to ooze from it, setting up a shark-attracting slick.*

Spreen. Chet does most of his fishing off southern California, and when the water temperature ranges between 59 and 66 degrees he knows there'll be big thresher sharks cruising along the kelp beds, anxious to latch onto an unsuspecting yellowtail or other forage.

The beauty of fishing for thresher sharks off southern California is that they're often located just a couple of miles from shore, where they leisurely satisfy their appetites on the huge quantities of forage that are available among the kelp beds. Kelp beds, for those of you who may not have fished them, are best described as underwater forests. It's not the same as the seaweed found along the Atlantic and Gulf coasts that drifts with the current. Kelp grows much like a tree, with a huge, thick trunk and giant leaves that fan out from the base. Some kelp beds are so thick that you can't maneuver a boat through them. The key is that the kelp provides protection for tiny sardines and anchovies that seek the sanctuary it offers. Yellowtail, Pacific barracuda, kelp bass, and sand bass in turn move in to feed on the sardines and anchovies, and the thresher sharks and leopard sharks aren't far behind.

It makes for interesting fishing, for while you're targeting sharks, it always pays to have a light outfit available with a small hook bait to cast to any of the smaller game and food fish that you spot working along the edges of the kelp. Many are fine table fare.

When Chet doesn't find sharks along the kelp beds, he'll move offshore a bit and try to find concentrations of anchovies. He'll often seek out his favorite bait purveyor, find out just where the bait boats have been successful in netting live anchovies, and then move to that area to set up for the threshers. Much as is the case on the Atlantic coast, he looks for a temperature break. Often there'll be a surface slick accompanied by markedly different water color, and it pays to investigate both sides of the temperature break; often within just a short distance you'll find a difference of from 5 to 8 degrees in water temperature, preferably in the 60-to-66-degree range. It's along the temperature break that the small baitfish congregate, followed by the Pacific barracuda, yellowtail, and other species, which the thresher sharks zero in on. Chet's favorite situation for locating schooling thresher sharks is to use a satellite temperature chart, and where he locates a hurricane-like eye of swirling water accompanied by a temperature break he knows the sharks will be there.

Big thresher sharks are found from Baja all the way north to Santa Barbara Island, including Punta Banda Bank, Upper Finger Bank, the Todos Santos area, Coronado Canyon, and 9-Mile Bank. The La Jolla Canyon also produces many threshers, as does the Dana Point area. I've scored well while sailing from Newport Beach, working the offshore banks where huge schools of sardines are often encountered. The prime forage species of the magnificent thresher shark are anchovies, sardines, mackerel, and bonito. While it may be an oversimplification to say so, where you find huge schools of these prime forage species you're guaranteed to find thresher sharks close at hand, responding to either trolled lures or baits, or succumbing to baits drifted back in a chum line.

Captain Steve James spends a great deal of time fishing the famous Stellwagen Bank north of Cape Cod, where porbeagle sharks congregate. The veteran Massachusetts skipper has many parties that fish for codfish and other bottom feeders from his charter rig *Quality Time*. He's learned that where you find codfish, you're certain to find porbeagle and other sharks, for the cod are a plentiful and easy meal for marauding sharks. The porbeagles like cold water, in the 40-to-64-degree range, and are available at a season of the year when most charter fishermen are seeking cod and haddock. Knowing that the sharks will provide bonanza fishing, Steve regularly sets out a shark rig while targeting the cod. His favorite bait is a mackerel with its head cut off and a single hook placed through the meaty part of its back, just behind the dorsal fin facing toward the tail with the point exposed.

Steve often fishes for cod in 225 to 300 feet of water. As he drifts along he'll be alert to signs that porbeagles are in the area. The best indicator is having a big codfish literally bitten in half as it's drawn to the surface. Often, however, a porbeagle will be visually observed following a hooked cod as it's brought to boatside.

In either case, this becomes the signal for Steve to set out the shark rig, which he sends into the depths and fishes approximately 50 to 75 feet off the bottom. This appears to be the depth at which the porbeagles cruise, feeding on forage such as mackerel and herring, which hold in schools at various depths in the water column. Frequently they'll descend to the bottom, where any struggling cod or haddock becomes an easy meal.

Fishing for porbeagle sharks off the Massachusetts coast begins in late May and continues through July, although there's no doubt they're in residence later into the season as well, despite the fact that most sportfishing interest at that time turns to the great opportunities for the bluefin tuna, yellowfin tuna, bigeye tuna, and albacore that invade these offshore waters. Toward this end, even when you may be targeting the tunas, don't hesitate to put out a couple of shark rigs; use a Snap Float to set the baits at a desired depth. Often you'll be pleasantly surprised by runoffs from sharks, as they like to linger in the areas where the tuna are plentiful, always ready to devour a tuna being fought by an angler.

Captain John Williams is a familiar fixture at Hoffman's Marina in Brielle, New Jersey. It's from there that he sails his charter boat *Blue Chip* from Manasquan Inlet and heads east to such fertile shark grounds as the Chicken Canyon, the Triple Wrecks, and even as far as the Hudson Canyon. John believes in fishing the structure that all these places provide, where the canyons, lumps, rock piles, and ridges cause baitfish to congregate.

Upon mention of baitfish, most anglers immediately think of mackerel, herring, and the like. John thinks big. His baitfish are the huge bluefish that move into area waters during May to spend the summer and much of the fall. Many of these bluefish weigh from 15 to 18 pounds and constitute a major portion of the mako shark's diet from spring until fall.

As such, John makes it a point to always have a supply of freshly caught bluefish on board, as they are his favorite bait when seeking makos, especially big makos. His anglers have landed many mako sharks in the 300-to-450-pound class, the majority of which succumbed to huge fillets of bluefish, or whole bluefish, used as bait.

John is not averse to capitalizing on another person's efforts to help him locate sharks. He's always on the lookout for the dragger fleets, for as they drag their nets they injure many fish, some of which escape from the nets and become an easy meal. As the draggers bring aboard the targeted species, they shovel crushed fish and undesirable species overboard. At such times it's not unusual to observe thousands of birds and gulls screaming and diving as they pick up the trash. Meanwhile, cutting the surface are the fins of a variety of sharks, including mako, thresher, tiger, and blue sharks, all of which have come to dine on the smorgasbord.

While the draggers present great angling opportunities, make certain you don't interfere with their pattern of working a particular area. The work of commercial fishermen is hazardous to begin with; the last thing they need is a sportfishing boat getting too close to or interfering with their efforts.

As I perused logbooks in preparing to write this chapter, I noted that draggers played an important role in much of the shark fishing I did along the Gulf coast, especially with respect to where to find sharks. The shelf waters are many miles from shore, and most shark fishing efforts are concentrated in the areas worked by shrimp draggers. The majorities of the shrimp draggers work through the night, then anchor and cull their catch, shoveling overboard crabs, crushed shrimp, squid, and a wide variety of fish that are caught in the trawl. Sharks regularly move in behind an anchored dragger to dine on the feast that is provided each morning.

Often in exchange for a couple of six-packs of Budweiser, a trawler crew will provide us with a 20- or 30-gallon container of the trash, which we subsequently use as chum. Indeed, I recall sev-

*Sharks tend to follow commercial draggers seeking bottom fish, scallops, and squid. When the nets are drawn they feed extensively on the trash shoveled overboard. It was while fishing among dragger discards that Al Ristori hooked the big blue shark he's fighting 45 miles southeast of Montauk Point, New York.*

eral instances when I saw huge bull sharks cruising just beneath the surface as the trawler crew passed over a bucket of the tasty delights!

While fishing just a few miles west of Redfish Pass on Florida's Gulf coast we scored while anchored near a mammoth spring hole where at the time jewfish were a legal target—they're now on the protected list—but bull sharks provided equally tough sport on the 30-pound outfits when the targeted species wouldn't cooperate.

I've also experienced excellent shark fishing while sailing from Pensacola, Florida,

*This bonnethead shark was hooked in water barely a foot deep. Many of the sharks that frequent the southern flats, such as blacktip sharks and sandbar sharks, can be caught while sight casting with spinning and fly tackle.*

and Mobile, Alabama, where we basically fished the same grounds as the party boats, popularly called "head boats" in that area. We were targeting red snapper and grouper but also fished live jacks on shark rigs set in the rod holders. At regular intervals the scream of a reel's ratchet would signal that a bull or brown shark had inhaled the jack that had been sending out a distress signal.

The color of the water off Grand Isle, Louisiana is unlike any I've ever experienced elsewhere. The flowage of the Mississippi River into the delta provides huge quantities of nutrients that, when coupled with the mud-laden flow, give a coloration to the water that at best can be described as murky. While this has resulted in many dead zones where marine life cannot survive, there are times when the water adjacent to these dead zones is laden with fish that have vacated the less-than-desirable water. Oxygen plays a key role, and where the demarcation lies you'll often find the forage. That's where the sharks will be as well, primarily because the forage, game, and food fish have all moved in concert out of the oxygen-starved water.

Fishing 30 to 40 miles out in the Gulf off Grand Isle, I've observed a shear demarcation line between the murky inshore water and the cobalt-blue water of offshore. Often this color change is accompanied by a temperature break, and frequently there's a weed line heavily populated with a variety of jacks, blue runners, dolphin, and other forage. It's not unusual to observe the distinct dorsal and

*Anglers trying their luck from party boats fishing the kelp beds off Ensenada, Mexico, often encounter sharks. A live baitfish cast toward the kelp often brings strikes from the sharks cruising along its perimeter, waiting for an unsuspecting baitfish to venture forth.*

tail fins of sharks as they cruised the edge of the weed line in search of an unsuspecting or lingering fish.

I've observed much the same distinct color change between inshore and offshore water off Hatteras, North Carolina, although not as drastic as off the Mississippi Delta. Because so many great game fish, including white and blue marlin, yellowfin tuna, wahoo, and dolphin, abound in the waters off Hatteras, little attention is paid to the abundant sharks. Here too, as almost everywhere, you'll find the sharks along the edge where there is a clear distinction between inshore and offshore waters, usually accompanied by a temperature break, and especially along the forage-laden weed lines where they know an easy meal is always available.

If ever there was an individual who has a love affair with sharks it's Pete Barrett, senior editor of the well-known *Fisherman* magazine, the bible of shark anglers along the middle and north Atlantic coast. Pete's beautiful Scarborough, the *Linda B,* has long been a familiar fixture on the offshore scene. A couple of decades back Pete wrote *Fishing for Sharks,* the definitive work on this exciting pastime. I'm duty-bound to admit that I gleaned many tips from his fine book over the years, and I make mention of this because it's especially important to absorb all that you can, especially about where to find sharks.

Veteran shark anglers like Pete and many others willingly share their knowledge of the offshore grounds and often make mention of those seemingly insignificant observations that can make the difference between success and failure when you're seeking sharks.

Pete believes in location, and maintains detailed logs of loran and GPS coordinates, but in each instance the water temperature and availability of forage play important roles. While a spot may have provided bonanza fishing last year—say, during the height of a bluefish or mackerel run—should this year's ocean currents cause the forage species to move to other locales, seeking the sharks there will be a lost cause. They simply won't be there, but instead will be hard on the tails of the swift-traveling mackerel and bluefish, their pièce de résistance.

*Bob Rosko handles the leader wire as Joe Basilio brings a blue shark alongside while fishing the productive shark grounds off Block Island, Rhode Island. The sharks invade these waters to feed on the abundance of cod, pollack, whiting, and other bottom fish that frequent the area.*

While Pete's *Linda B* seeks tuna and billfish as the season progresses, he's not averse to seeking sharks in the Mud Hole off New Jersey or the many wrecks such as the *Virginia* and *Lillian* when the canyon sport sometimes slumps during the height of summer. He knows from experience that the Mud Hole wrecks have a huge population of ling, with bluefish often in the upper strata of the water column, while the inshore wrecks have an abundance of sea bass, cunners, and the ever-present bluefish hovering above them.

In any of these offshore waters, don't hesitate to investigate any activity of scallop draggers. As the draggers draw their trawls they bring up huge quantities of not only crabs, shrimp, and fish but scallops as well. In addition to discarding the trash—which attracts primarily smaller fish and, in turn, sharks—the draggers also have crews on board who work at low tables shucking scallops. The shells and stomachs are dumped overboard, all of which provides a feeding station and keeps packs of marauding sharks close at hand.

The single most important consideration in locating sharks— whether you fish the Atlantic, Pacific, or Gulf coast—is that sharks require a very great deal of forage to satisfy their insatiable appetites. Where you find huge schools of sardines off Newport Beach, California, you're certain to find threshers. If it's on Stellwagen Bank off Massachusetts, you just know porbeagles will be in residence when the herring, mackerel, and cod are plentiful. Much the same can be said if you're targeting mako sharks at the Triple Wrecks off New Jersey when the big bluefish arrive each spring. Along the Gulf coast the big brown and bull sharks are certain to be close at hand on the reefs that hold red snapper and grouper. The salmon sharks of Alaska are no exception, and where you find the salmon, the sharks that carry their name won't be far behind.

By all means maintain a logbook of your shark fishing exploits, for their movements and the grounds they frequent can be tracked from season to season with utmost certainty. Yet the tracking of the forage is perhaps more important, for sharks will be following in short order.

*Captain Frank Fuhr of the* Reel One *likes to use a bluefish fillet on a two-hook rig, with a fluorescent orange plastic skirt to give the bait a tantalizing action as it's drifted along. He adjusts the Snap Float from time to time to fish the bait at various depths in the water column, permitting the float to drift 100 or more feet from the boat, well back in the chum line.*

# 7

# Chumming

The keen sense of smell that sharks possess readily attracts them to any source of food found in the sea. They will dine on lively fresh tuna and bluefish, viciously slashing them to pieces, or relish ripping chunks from a dead whale or porpoise floating on the surface that you could smell a quarter mile away. They aren't as omnivorous and indiscriminate as their reputations seem to indicate. They are, however, the keepers of the seas, cleaning up whatever's edible, including sea lions and walruses. Indeed, at one time or another I suspect a piece of every living thing in the sea has been removed from the stomach of a shark.

Chumming, using ground fish or tiny pieces of fish, is unquestionably the most effective method sportfishermen use to catch sharks. Because of their acute ability to smell even the tiniest quantity of food, they readily respond to a chum line that may have drifted a mile or more from where it originated, ultimately moving to the source. They know that eventually they'll find the source, and an easy meal . . . or hopefully your hook bait!

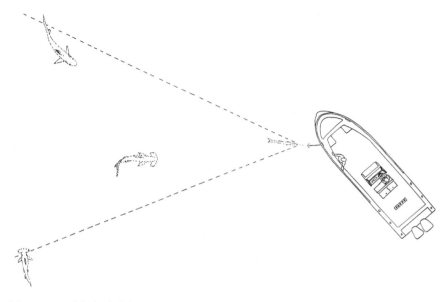

*Many successful shark fishermen obtain a bucket of carcasses from dockside fish markets and tie off several tuna or bluefish carcasses as they chum and drift. The carcasses quickly begin to deteriorate, with tiny pieces separating from the bones, all the while emitting a strong scent that attracts sharks within range of hook baits.*

Chumming for most species of fish, such as tuna, bluefish, white sea bass, and other game fish, results in dispensing overboard small quantities of forage, like chunks of butterfish or menhaden, or whole live fish such as anchovies or sardines, to attract the fish. Were you to try this approach when chumming for sharks, you'd find that the finned chopping machines would often set well back in the chum line and simply feed on the food being dropped into the sea, well beyond your hook baits, leisurely swimming off when their bellies were full.

Chumming is most often done from a drifting boat, with the drift planned to carry the craft and its chum line over areas regularly frequented by sharks (as discussed in chapter 6).

Sometimes, however, you'll find vast areas of barren ocean, with the exception of isolated lumps or ridges, coupled with rocky outcroppings where sharks are known to frequent to feed on the abundant forage. In such locations it's far more effective to anchor your craft, positioning it so the chum is carried toward the bottom conformation where the sharks may be feeding.

Much the same holds true around deep-water wrecks and artificial reefs. The wreck or other structure attracts bottom feeders, which in turn are an easy meal for the sharks. The structure often attracts herring, mackerel, or other forage species that settle into the midrange of the water column. The sharks often take up permanent residence in close proximity to the wreck or other natural bottom structure and stay so long as the forage stays, only vacating the area as the forage species or bottom feeders leave, at which time the sharks often follow them on their migration trek.

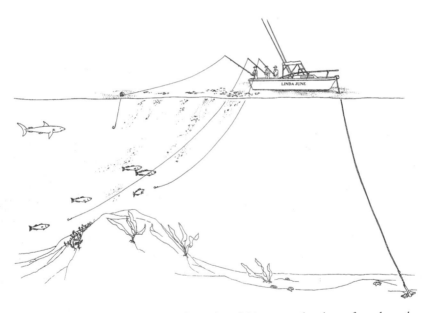

*The author regularly puts out a shark bait when fishing around rocks, reefs, and wrecks for other species such as tuna and bluefish. The shark line regularly results in a bonus catch, as the sharks are in the area because there's a plentiful supply of tuna, blues, and the forage on which they're feeding to satisfy their appetite.*

## CHUMMING TECHNIQUES
The first step in preparing for an offshore shark chumming excursion is obtaining chum. There are those sharkers who prefer fresh-

ground chum from species such as menhaden, mackerel, herring, or mullet. They feel the fresh chum is more potent than frozen chum, although I can't say that I've ever had any problem while attracting sharks with frozen chum. Indeed, I've found that the latter has several advantages.

Ground chum is available at marinas all along the coast and usually provided in plastic 3- to 5-gallon buckets. For a typical eight-hour day of actual chumming you'll usually require two or three 5-gallon buckets of the odoriferous concoction. I prefer the frozen, as I then transfer it to another 5-gallon bucket that I've modified to act as an automated chummer by placing a dozen or more 2-inch-diameter holes in it.

Chunks of frozen chum are transferred to the chum bucket, its lid is placed on, and it's suspended overboard via a ¼-inch rope tied to the bucket's handle and secured to a stern cleat. The rocking motion of the boat, along with an occasional yank on the rope, caus-

*Many anglers simply insert a can of frozen chum upside down in a plastic storage box and suspend it overboard via a rope attached to a cleat. As the chum thaws, the movement of the boat causes it to ooze from the slits in the box, establishing an unbroken slick.*

es the thawing chum to ooze from the bucket as you drift along, establishing a long, unbroken chum line.

Some anglers use a similar technique in that they employ a plastic storage container—much like those used to transport cartons of milk—and attach a series of ropes to each of its four sides. A 5-gallon pail of frozen chum is placed upside down in the container, and it's tied off at the stern, where the chum oozes from it.

I have used both methods and prefer the bucket with holes drilled in it over the plastic storage container. The key to chumming is maintaining an unbroken chum line, and the automatic chum bucket accomplishes this with ease. Often in the excitement of fishing or after hours of no action, anglers become complacent, and for whatever the reason the chumming operation is neglected; the shark-attracting potential of the chum is diminished. With the automated system of the chum bucket constantly oozing chum, however, the lack of a person handling the chumming detail ceases to be a problem.

## The Chumsicle

Still another unique method of automatically chumming is one that I believe was first developed to attract sharks to boats used by scuba divers. Off Walkers Cay in the Bahamas, a dive boat operator began collecting the carcasses of fish that were cleaned. The carcasses and stomach contents included snappers and groupers from the reefs, along with dolphin and wahoo brought in from offshore and any other fish that were cleaned at the dock.

The assorted carcasses, blood, stomachs, skin, and fish scraps were collected in a plastic 20-gallon barrel. When the barrel was filled, which easily happened daily as the charter and private boats returned to the dock, a 20-foot-long piece of ½-inch nylon rope with three or four large overhand knots in the end was inserted well into the bucket. The entire bucket of carcasses, with 2 feet of the knotted end inserted in it, was then placed in the freezer for a couple of days.

On leaving for the shark grounds, the bucket was placed aboard the boat. By the time the fishing grounds were reached, the bucket

*Sharks often set up and feed on the discards of offshore draggers that are fishing for bottom fish, scallops, squid, or shrimp. It's wise to get to know the commercial skippers, for often they can key you in on the location of schools of sharks, and provide you some discards, as is being done here off Montauk, Long Island.*

of carcasses usually had thawed sufficiently so that the entire frozen block could be removed from it. The rope was then attached to a stern cleat and the frozen block of carcasses tossed overboard. Because the rope was frozen and held secure by the knots within the frozen carcasses, the block would remain securely fastened to it until the last bit of carcasses and entrails thawed.

Some sharkers would attach a 2-foot-diameter marker buoy to a 100-foot length of anchor line and permit it to drift with the boat, occasionally slowly pulling in the frozen mass and the congregation of fish and sharks feeding on it, whereupon they'd slip out the oldest, smelliest bait on the boat. This was promptly engulfed by a hungry shark.

Nicknamed a "chumsicle," the practice was quickly adapted by shark fishermen. When placed in the water, the chumsicle begins to thaw and immediately begins to attract small fish such as jacks, blue runners, grunts, and other palm-sized fish. Soon bigger fish move in to enjoy the buffet, with snappers and groupers rising from the reef if inshore, and king mackerel, dolphin, and wahoo raiding the chumsicle when offshore. Often it's only a matter of minutes before there's a collection of half a dozen or more species feeding on the thawing carcasses, skin, and stomachs.

As you watch the scene develop you'll be surprised that the fish aren't attacking one another. There appears to be a pecking order: The fish will circle about, with some picking up the scraps that drift away while the sharks viciously attack the chumsicle, literally clenching their jaws to the thawing mass of decaying food and thrashing wildly as they try to rip pieces of the partially thawed fish from the main block.

At such times drifting a chunk bait or fillet to the sharks usually will bring a quick strike. It's interesting to note that the sharks won't be bothering the grunts, snappers, jacks, and blue runners swimming about. However, I've often caught these small baitfish on a tiny leadhead jig, quickly slipped a shark hook into the live bait, and drifted it back toward the chumsicle. Invariably a shark would immediately depart from the chum and zero in on the live hook bait, attracted to the distress signals it was emitting. It appears that while the scent of the thawing carcasses and stomachs is what attracts the sharks in the first place, these predators just can't resist the urge to devour a struggling forage fish emitting distress signals.

While the chumsicle is used primarily in tropical waters, I've tried it on a smaller scale in northeast canyons, using the carcasses of bluefish, tuna, sea bass, fluke, and other fish that I collected at dockside from party and charter boat mates when they returned from offshore. It's a very effective method, with the only drawback being the need for a large, walk-in-type cooler to store and freeze the 20-gallon plastic containers.

There are also electronic chumming machines on the market, into which whole fish are fed and then ground and dispensed overboard automatically with a timer, although I've never had an opportunity to use one.

It's always a good practice to carry an extra slab or box of whole baitfish such as menhaden, mackerel, mullet, or butterfish for use as hook baits. I also like to spice up the ground chum—which sharks can taste and smell, but can't actually eat because it's so small—with very small, finger-sized chunks cut from the whole fish.

I like to use a serrated knife to cut the chunks while the baits are partially thawed, which makes the job easier. I'll cut up at least a 5-gallon pail of the small chunks, having them all set to dispense once the fishing grounds are reached. It's important, however, to keep in mind that these chunks will just supplement the ground chum; they're used to entice and excite the sharks to continue moving toward the source, not to feed them. Even the biggest shark has a limit as to how much it can eat, and too liberal a chum line of chunks will hurt your chance of success.

If the port you're sailing from is in close proximity to a fishing spot where you can catch a handful of live baits, by all means do so. You'll need a live well to keep them in good condition, or can jury-

*Often there's a strong current offshore, which tends to balloon live baits toward the surface as you drift along. To get the bait to the desired depth you can often attach an ordinary trolling sinker to the line using an elastic band or dental floss, which breaks off once a shark is hooked.*

rig a round 10- or 20-gallon pail in the cockpit in which to keep the baits, aerating the water with the boat's saltwater washdown pump.

In the Florida Keys many skippers stop over a reef and use small hooks and tiny baits to catch several yellowtail snappers, grunts, blue runners, or jack crevalle, all of which make excellent hook baits and also work as live decoys. Off the northeast coast it's not uncommon to watch the electronic fishfinder on the way to the offshore grounds and, once a school of mackerel is located, to stop and jig several of the 2- to 3-pounders for the live well. Live bluefish are also easily caught live bait on which mako, porbeagle, thresher, and tiger sharks regularly feed. All of these baits make excellent live decoys in addition to hook baits.

## TACKLE AND LEADERS

I prefer rigging all my tackle before heading to the shark grounds. In this way I can be certain everything is in order and ready for a day's fishing, without having delays once the fishing grounds are reached. I am also very suspicious of friends bringing along their "favorite fishing outfit." Over a great many years of having fished for most of the major game fish in the world, I've observed more fish lost by anglers on my boats and others when they hooked a trophy fish on an outfit they used perhaps once a year. Improperly set drags, frozen reels, broken lines and rods occur so often that I strongly encourage my guests to use the boat's gear. All the *Linda June* outfits are identically matched, so you don't have to think when you pick up a rod. They're also all balanced outfits, with properly set drags, on reels that are meticulously maintained with lines regularly replaced.

I'm a near fanatic about having an uncluttered cockpit when shark fishing. The biggest problem I've observed on boats aboard which I've fished is too much clutter, including too many rods and reels, buckets, ropes, trash cans, tackle boxes, and gosh knows what else.

All I want to see in the cockpit are four outfits ready to fish.

This requires attention to detail before leaving dockside. Beginning with the basic outfits, you can use standard big-game trolling outfits, standard stand-up outfits, or light-tackle stand-up outfits with smaller reels filled with Spectra, Dyneema, or other types of fine-diameter braided line. I've known a few shark anglers who fished for big sharks with heavyweight spinning tackle, but I'm still from the old school that believes spinning is for casting. If you feel more comfortable with a fixed-spool reel, by all means make certain it's top quality and up to the task at hand. Suffice it to say that each rod, reel, and line should be thoroughly checked.

Sharks have a nasty habit of literally wrapping themselves in a line as they're being fought. I've had occasions when I had to cut 50 feet from the terminal end of the line after having landed a huge blue shark that was completely wrapped up in it. The result was that the monofilament line felt as though it had been sandpapered. Had I not cut back the line there's no question it would have broken as soon as pressure was brought to bear on the next shark. As a result, prior to every trip I run 50 to 75 feet of the terminal end of my line through my fingers to detect any abrasions, nicks, or spots that just don't feel right, and cut back accordingly.

Then I double the last 10 or 12 feet of line using a surgeon's loop or a Bimini twist, both of which are extremely strong. The double line is a bit of insurance enabling me to get several turns of line on the reel as I lead a shark alongside. This allows me to apply more pressure as the deckhand reaches for the wire leader.

I then use an offshore swivel knot or uniknot to tie on a 300-pound-test Sampo ball-bearing swivel with coastlock snap. It's also wise to slip a small piece of firm-fitting surgical tubing over the snap. This will prevent it from inadvertently opening, which has been known to happen, especially when a particularly nasty shark wraps up in the cable or wire. While the primary role of the swivel is to prevent line twist and the coastlock snap to attach the leader, it also is the first handhold a gloved deckhand grasps as he reaches for the leader to lead the shark within range of gaffing or release.

Opinions vary on the best way to construct a leader for shark fishing, with some devotees favoring single-strand stainless-steel wire, while others prefer stainless-steel cable. Over the years I've used both, and even used them in combination, and really never had any major problems with either. I've settled on the combination leader of half cable and half single strand, joined with a large swivel, as my preferred choice. This eliminates the need to take wraps on the leader when a big shark is at boatside, which is an extremely unsafe practice.

The breaking strength of the leader material will in large part be determined by the size of the sharks you're seeking. For the majority of pelagic sharks, leader materials testing between 250 and 600 pounds are more than adequate. There are specialists, however, who specifically seek out big hammerhead, mako, tiger and thresher sharks and who use upward of 600-pound-test cable, simply because they don't want to risk losing a fish due to a failure of the lighter tests.

For my purposes I've used 250-pound-test 49-strand stainless-steel cable and find it more than adequate. It balances well with the tackle I've employed over a period of many years. I know some charter skippers who won't use cable, claiming that big sharks can literally bite through it during a long fight, their slashing teeth breaking the fine strands one wire at a time until it fails. I can't say I've had that experience, but in fairness must say my catches couldn't begin to compare with those of the chartermen who are targeting sharks daily.

I begin making a leader by using two 7-foot-long pieces, one of cable and one of single-strand stainless-steel wire. A doubled loop is crimped to one end of the cable leader material, and a second doubled loop is attached to a 200-pound-test Spro or a Sampo ball-bearing swivel at the other end. I then take the piece of single-strand wire and use a haywire twist, finished with just two or three turns of a barrel twist, to attach it to the swivel. Finally the hook is attached to the terminal end of the leader with a haywire twist. I keep the barrel twist section that finishes up the haywire twist short, as the wire is less apt to break.

I've had 280-pound-test single-strand stainless-steel wire kink and break while fighting a shark. Here it becomes a matter of personal choice, with either material providing reliable service when properly balanced with the tackle being used. I rig the single-strand wire in two sections, much the same as the cable, and use a haywire twist to make the connections.

I've found the two-sectioned leader beneficial when a shark is brought alongside. This is especially true since we're amateur fishermen, and not accustomed to handling 12- to 14- or even 20-foot-long leaders as used by many charter boat skippers and their mates. With the large swivel separating the two sections, it's easier to get a second handhold, especially when attempting to cut the leader in order to release the shark. There's also the peripheral benefit that line twist is minimized with the two swivels as you drift along.

Another option is that of using wind-on leaders. My good friend Jeff Merrill, a noted sportfishing writer who hunts sharks with a passion, in recent years has used wind-on leaders exclusively. He is devoted to tag and release and finds that the wind-on leader made of 250-pound-test monofilament works extremely well. It can be reeled right through the guides, enabling the angler to reel until the swivel reaches the rod's tip-top. This puts the shark within easy range for tagging and cutting the leader.

The prime advantage with the wind-on leader is the avoidance of a wireman having to grab a leader. As anyone who has fished for big sharks knows, having several hundred pounds of wild, thrashing shark at the side of the boat makes for a dangerous situation. By all means avoid taking wraps on the leader.

Jeff spools 80-pound-test Dacron on his Penn 50TW International and doubles 2 to 3 feet of the terminal end of the line to form a loop. He then loops the wind-on section of the monofilament leader, which is fitted within another looped section of Dacron, forming an ideal loop-to-loop connection that easily passes through the tip-top and guides.

Because he uses heavy, 250-pound-test monofilament as leader material, he finishes off the leader using a crimp, to which his wire leader is attached. However, to ensure that the crimp doesn't get jammed in the rod tip when retrieving, he first adds a large plastic bead to the swivel. This prevents him from inadvertently reeling the crimped leader into the rod's tip-top. Some anglers attach a 5-inch long piece of red ribbon to the terminal crimp or swivel, which alerts them to stop reeling.

# HOOKS

Quite honestly, years ago when we went shark fishing we often used old hooks that showed signs of rust and were removed from trolling feathers and other lures. They were for the most part forged O'Shaughnessy hooks ranging in size from 8/0 through 12/0. We used them because we felt they were more than adequate to hold sharks of up to several hundred pounds, and would easily rust away when the shark was cut free.

In those days everybody religiously filed their hooks to a needle-sharp point, as right-out-of-the-box hooks generally had dull points. All that's changed today. Now shark fishermen have a fine assortment of excellent hooks from which to make a selection. Today's hooks are laser-sharpened, which results in a very strong point, and they're chemically treated to give them a finish that is resistant to salt water and its corrosive tendency. Where hooks of the past required sharpening, were you to sharpen a hook manufactured with today's technology you would actually damage its effectiveness! No need to use a file.

While every major hook manufacturer in the business shudders at the thought of putting a file to a new hook, there are still fishermen who prefer to do so. As recently as when preparing this book I spoke with two veteran shark anglers, one of whom swore by using a file to sharpen his hooks, while the other swore at the notion of ever sharpening them. One felt the extremely sharp hook ensures quick penetration, while the other was convinced that if a file-sharpened hook hit the teeth in a shark's jaw it would be apt to bend and fail to hook the fish—in which case the file-sharpened hook often rips too large a hole in the jaw. The latter could result in a lost shark midway through the battle.

I've employed Mustad, Eagle Claw, Owner, and Gamakatsu hooks over the years, and they're all fine quality. Each has particular attributes that find favor among sharkers, and it all comes down to what you find a comfort level with. Some anglers swear by ringed hooks, while others prefer needle-eye hooks. I prefer the needle-eye models myself, as there's no chance of the leader wrapping up on the eye of a ringed hook. The needle eye also makes for ease while rigging baits.

The Mustad 7699 is one of the most popular hook styles in use along the coast. Eagle Claw's L9015 also finds popularity with many anglers, as does Owner's Live Bait style, a Pacific coast favorite. Tag-and-release anglers especially favor Gamakatsu's Circle hook style 210422, which facilitates quick release because the shark is often hooked in the corner of the jaw.

Keep an assortment of sizes on board, ranging from 8/0 through 12/0. Some rig their baits with 16/0 hooks when they're seeking record-breaking sharks in the 500-pound-plus class. I was aboard boats years ago that used shark hooks so mammoth they had no size designation; looking like meat hooks, they were attached to a piece of chain and fished from a piece of manila rope with a live 12-pound little tunny as bait!

## TERMINAL TACKLE

Making leaders is a great wintertime project, as you can leisurely prepare them without the pressure of having to hurry to the fishing grounds. I usually package each rig in a zipper-lock plastic bag, and know that when I reach into the tackle locker for a leader it's exactly what I want. The only variation will be the size of the hook, usually from 8/0 through 12/0.

Toward this end, if you're new to shark fishing and aren't yet comfortable preparing your own leaders, I suggest finding a reputable tackle shop along the coast that specializes in preparing quality terminal gear for sharks. Take care to avoid the shop that hurriedly takes a swivel, length of leader wire, and hook, makes a couple of quick haywire twists, and sends you off shark fishing.

For many years I've dealt with the Reel Seat in Brielle, New Jersey. Dave Arbeitman and Grant Toman own the shop. Both are close friends, and for many years I've turned to their expertise in producing fine terminal gear when time didn't permit me to prepare my own rigs, spreader bars, and leaders. They both take great pride in their work, and they try not to complicate matters for their customers.

They believe in keeping it plain and simple, and have settled on four standard rigs for their clientele. Their most popular shark rig is a two-hook model made with 9/0 or 10/0 Mustad 7699 welded-eye offset hooks, which works great with a fillet cut from a big bluefish or with a whole mackerel. It's crimped with precision to 275- or 480-pound-test cable and finished off with a hunter orange skirt that moves enticingly through the water as it's drifted along. It was Dave who began using the skirts—the same kind used on many trolling lures—years ago, and he attributes much of his success to their action when used in conjunction with a fillet bait.

Their three other rigs are:

- 240-pound-test coffee-colored stainless-steel leader material, employing haywire twists, finished off with minimal barrel twist and broken cleanly, with a Mustad 7699 hook.

- A combination rig utilizing half 480-pound-test cable, joined via a Spro or Sampo big-game swivel to an equal length of 240-pound-test coffee-colored stainless-steel leader material and a Mustad 7699 hook.

- A rig using a size 12/0 Gamakatsu 210422, heavy-duty Live Bait hook. This style aids in the releasing of sharks, as most are hooked in the corner of the jaw. This is rigged on 275- or 480-pound-test coffee-colored cable leader material.

All three of these rigs can also be made up in double-hook models, depending on the size and species of shark being sought or found in a particular area.

I can't stress enough that the rigs be made up properly, from the correct crimping of cable to the careful preparation of haywire twists and using hook styles that consistently stand up under the tremendous strain of shark fishing, and don't fail you after a long battle.

You can even custom-order your leaders from Dave and Grant, specifying Owner, Mustad, Eagle Claw, Gamakatsu, or other hook brands of your choice. Some anglers prefer to have rattles added to their leaders, as they give out a tantalizing noise when the rocking motion of the boat moves them through the water, adding to their appeal.

## Floats and Sinkers

A couple of other items you'll find necessary are a supply of floats and sinkers. The former suspend baits at a desired level during the drift; the latter send the baits deeper when a fast drift tends to pull them toward the upper level of the water column.

Over a period of many years I've used cork and Styrofoam floats to suspend baits at a desired level, and also used inflated balloons, all of which served their purpose. The one drawback is that they are environmentally unacceptable. Seabirds and fish often ingest them after they've broken free of fishing line, which can lead to their demise.

A product that solves the float problem is the Snap Float, made by Aqua Gem. Developed by entrepreneur Jim Kaczynski of Connecticut, it's a unique float system built of durable plastic and rugged stainless steel. The hinged float is placed on the line and held in position by heavy-duty elastic bands. When a shark or other game fish assaults the bait, the elastics slip off and the Snap Float slides along the line, not handicapping you as you fight a shark. When the shark is landed or released, the float is easily reset.

A great advantage of the Snap Float is its developer's recognition that a sizable float is needed, especially when you want to send a bait into the depths and there is a strong drift caused by current or wind. Jim's No. 36 float will suspend up to 12 ounces of weight, including bait and sinker, while his No. 39 supports fully 20 ounces of weight. This is very important, for without adequate weight it's virtually impossible to fish the bait at the desired depth. Ideally, with a leisurely drift, the line between float and bait should be perpendicular to the bottom.

The floats are available in bright colors including hot pink, yellow, and pale green, all easily seen as they bob on the surface 50 to 100 feet from the boat.

The most popular sinker style while shark chumming is the bank, with a dipsey a close second. Most shark fishermen use a piece of dental floss to tie their sinker to the Sampo swivel where it's tied to the line. During a fight with a big shark the dental floss will break, and the sinker is lost. The sinker should be heavy enough so that the line is perpendicular as you ease the bait to the desired depth. If it streams too far out, just use a heavier sinker. It's best to carry sizes ranging from 6 to 20 ounces on board, which will cover all but the most severe weather conditions.

## LET'S GO FISHING!

With chum on board, a supply of both live and dead baits, four identical outfits all rigged and ready, and an ample supply of hooks and leaders, floats, and sinkers, you're ready to go!

One of the last things I religiously do prior to heading for the offshore grounds is check the weather report. With today's Internet technology, it's easy to check local weather and the sea conditions at offshore buoys strategically located off the coast. Check the long-range forecast of the weather channels, and watch the radar for signs of any approaching low-pressure front that will result in bad weather offshore. It's important to remember that the weather when you sail isn't as important as what it will be like 8 to 24 hours later. You certainly don't want to pound your way back through heavy weather from the offshore canyons 100 miles at sea. It's bad enough when you inadvertently get caught offshore with bad weather. Bottom line: If the weather's iffy, remain at the dock!

Monitoring the weather will prove important as you plot your destination. For in chumming for sharks you'll be positioning yourself to drift through an area known to have either structure, large concentrations of forage, a break in water temperature, or a warm core eddy being swept in from offshore. In an ideal situation you may encounter all of the above. That's why it's so important to know the anticipated wind direction, so you can plan your drift to travel over what may be miles of choice water. You want to use wind and current to your advantage, establishing an unbroken chum line that can extend for miles, its distinctive scent attracting sharks to your hook baits.

By being prepared with a sea anchor, you can deploy it immediately on reaching the fishing grounds if the wind is strong and the drift fast. In this way you don't have to waste time and react later; you're set right from the beginning. I know of several shark fishermen who religiously deploy the sea anchor, for they prefer a lazy drift in which the chum settles deep and the boat moves along slowly, with the parachute slowing its drift considerably.

On reaching the fishing grounds, I always make a point of noting the loran or GPS coordinates where I'm beginning my drift and the water temperature. I'll often use this information later in the day as I prepare for another drift. The information also alerts me as to when we drift through a temperature break, identifying exactly where it occurs. I turn on the fishfinder as well, not so much to find sharks as to observe bait concentrations or schools of game fish frequenting the area as we drift along.

## Establishing the Chum Line

The first order of business is establishing the chum line. If we've done our homework at dockside, this is an easy task. Fill the 5-gallon chum bucket with holes in it with several large chunks of frozen menhaden, herring, mackerel, or other ground fish chum. To add to the potency of the chum, many anglers pour on bunker oil, which adheres to the ground chum as it disperses. Secure the cover on the bucket, attach the rope to a stern clean, then deposit the automatic chum bucket in the water.

You'll immediately notice that tiny pieces of chum will begin to exit the chum bucket from the holes. Some will settle while others drift on the surface, the oil leaving a distinct trace. On a calm day you can literally observe a light slick on the surface as you drift along. This unbroken slick, and the tiny particles of chum drifting beneath it, is what will get the sharks moving to you.

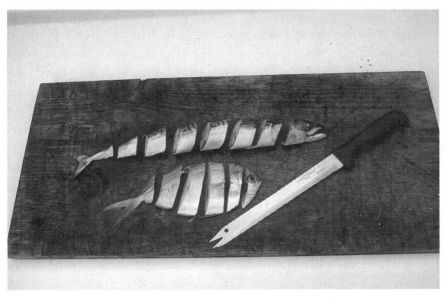

*It's helpful to supplement the ground chum with small chunks cut from whatever species are available. Included here are mackerel and butterfish, cut into pieces that will whet the appetite of a shark yet not feed it, making it more responsive to a larger bait drifted back in the chum line.*

While some sharkers use only ground chum, other will spice the ground with small chunks. Should you elect to use chunks of butterfish, bunker, mackerel, anchovies, or sardines, do so sparingly. Toss a handful at regular intervals. Keep in mind that while you're targeting sharks, the tiny pieces of ground chum will often attract baitfish and squid, which in turn often attract bonito and tuna into the slick as well. You'll also observe seabirds and Mother Carey's chicks in the area. Porpoises and whales are also observed frequently, all good signs—for where the ocean is busy with sea life the sharks are certain to be close at hand.

## Setting Lines

When fishing from any of our three *Linda June*s we found that keeping three lines in the water was most effective. Using more lines than this often results in tangles, and on occasion resulted in a royal mess once a shark was hooked and the lines weren't cleared quickly enough. A fourth outfit is rigged and baited up for those frequent occasions when a shark moves up the chum line, targeting the chum bucket, and along the way completely ignores the deep-set hook baits. We're ready to immediately slip a rigged bait to the marauder.

There are many variations on both dead and live baits and how to place them on your hook, and all of them produce at one time or another. What's important is that you begin with an offering of a variety of baits. Over a period of time you'll build a confidence level in the bait that gets the most strikes. It's human nature to drift toward what works best for you, which may be contrary to what is experienced by other shark fishermen.

I've had excellent results with fillets of fish as hook baits. Bonito, tuna, bluefish, and mackerel are all fine choices. I suspect the exposed meat of the fillet gives off more scent than a whole fish bait. Especially effective is a slab of fillet cut from a bluefish. Don't worry about the bait being too large; I've cut fillets from 10- and 12-pound bluefish and had them assaulted with a vengeance by hungry sharks.

Also, don't worry about bait being fresh. With so many species of fish there's great emphasis on using fresh bait to draw strikes. Not so with sharks, as the older and smellier the bait is, the more effective it can sometimes be. I recall a day when we were chumming for

*A pair of fillets cut from sardines, mackerel, herring, or bluefish make an attractive shark bait. The fillets flutter enticingly as they're drifted along, emitting an oily scent that attracts sharks.*

bluefin tuna with Fritz Hubner aboard his *Mistress Too* some 45 miles out of Montauk. A huge shark came up in the chum line and literally bit a 50-pound bluefin tuna in half. With that deckhand Pete Casale repaired to the ice chest, where he removed a hook bait used the previous day. It smelled to high heaven and was so soft I couldn't believe it would stay on the hook. Once put in the water it was engulfed in an instant by a blue shark that, when I released it at boatside was estimated to top 300 pounds!

Once you complete filleting the bluefish, tuna, bonito, or mackerel for bait, you should use the carcasses as an added attractor. Tie a piece of 130-pound-test Dacron around the tail of each carcass, then tie them off to the railing so they're suspended just beneath the

*In most types of fishing you want the freshest bait possible. Not so when shark fishing. Mate Pete Casale of the* Mistress Too *out of Montauk likes a bait that has a strong scent to it, as was the case with this bluefish fillet, which moments after this photo was taken resulted in a strike from a big blue shark.*

*It pays to carry a long-handled net with you when you go offshore and are shark fishing in an area frequented by commercial draggers. As they shovel overboard discards, often called trash, you can cruise along and scoop the floating dead fish from the surface, as the author did to fill the ice chest with a day's supply of fresh baits and chum.*

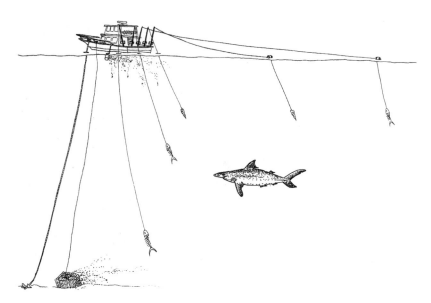

*In setting out your baited hooks, fish them at different levels in the water column for maximum results. Use fillets of fish, as well as carcasses, as bait. Disperse chum from a chum bucket tied off to the boat, and from a chum cage lowered to the bottom, which works effectively when anchored.*

surface at various locations around the boat. This adds to the scent being dispensed by the ground chum. I've often had sharks come up and grab the carcasses, at which time they can quickly be retrieved and the bait on the fourth outfit drifted, whereupon the sharks are onto it in an instant.

With big baits it pays to use a pair of hooks. I'll often rig a second hook by crimping a piece of 12-inch-long cable either to the eye of the first hook, or to the crimped loop in the cable. The same can easily be done if you're using stainless-steel leader wire. In fact, I've often used single-strand wire for the second hook, as it can be added right on the fishing grounds with ease.

Place the lead hook in the front of the fillet and the trailing hook in the center of the fillet. The fillet should lie flat as you place it in the water, so it doesn't spin as you drift along.

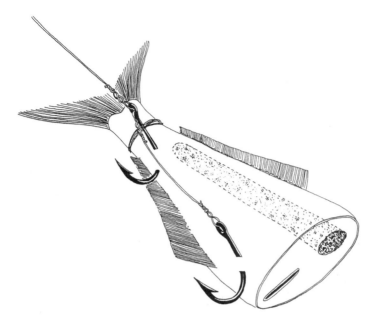

*Many shark fishermen favor a double-hook rig. A bait rigged in this manner won't spin as you drift along. To enhance the shark-attracting effectiveness of the bait, many anglers remove its backbone and stuff the cavity with chum.*

If there's a lazy, nominal drift you may not need a sinker, but if the wind and current are moving you along swiftly, now is the time to add a sinker as described earlier.

The first line in the water is the line set deepest. This can vary, depending on the depth of the water being fished and past experience. In far-offshore canyon waters I'll usually set the first bait around 175 feet down, and I secure the Snap Float at that depth. As you drift along, the depth of the bait may vary depending on the speed of the drift, anywhere from 175 to 150 feet deep.

Place the bait in the water until it reaches the desired depth, and then let the Snap Float carry it 100 to 125 feet from the boat. Placing the rod in a rod holder, set a very light strike drag—just enough that the line doesn't overrun or backlash when you get a pickup. Set the reel's ratchet to signal a strike. To prevent the line

*You need only a pair of outfits when chumming offshore for sharks. Make certain to fish each bait at a different depth in the water column, because sharks regularly move from the depths to the surface as they search for a meal, especially when attracted by the scent of ground chum.*

from wrapping around the rod tip in a rough ocean, many anglers will attach an outrigger clip to a piece of line secured at the reel seat. The line is then snapped into the outrigger clip, pulling free when there's a pickup. Some anglers even run the line to their outriggers, which serve the same purpose and give additional dropback as well.

The second bait can be rigged in the same manner, or you may choose to rig a live bait. I've used a couple of different techniques when rigging live baits. With tuna, bonito, or mackerel, which must constantly be swimming to stay alive, I've found that using a rigging needle and rigging twine, running it through their eye sockets, and

*Sharks will often bite through a baitfish, missing the hook if it's placed in the head. A good trick is to run the hook into the mouth, out the gills, and then back in the anus and out by the anal fin. An elastic band around the bait holds the wire or cable leader tight to the bait.*

then tying off the twine to the bend of the J-style hook works just fine. The bait will stay alive and active for a long while.

The only problem I've experienced with large live baits is that a shark will frequently bite the bait in half, engulfing one half and missing the hook completely. Sometimes the shark will return to the remaining half, so be patient before you reel in a bait that a shark has attacked.

With live bluefish I'll often use a two-hook rig, placing the first hook through the meaty part of the back, just behind the head. Use a rigging needle to run a piece of single-strand stainless-steel leader

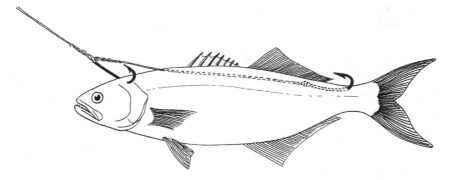

*A whole dead fish makes an effective bait when drifting for sharks. Use a rigging needle to run a second hook through the fleshy part of the back, exiting near the tail. This hooks many sharks that have a tendency to bite through a bait, missing a single hook rigged in the head.*

### HAYWIRE TWIST

*The haywire twist should be used to make a loop in the end of stainless-steel leader wire. The key is holding the wire securely and making the initial wraps of the wire around each other, and then finishing it off with a barrel wrap, laying the wire side by side around the standing part of the wire. Complete by making a short handle in the tag end of the wire and bending it back and forth, which will make a clean, neat break with no burr on which you might rip your hands. Never use pliers to finish it off, as this will leave a burr.*

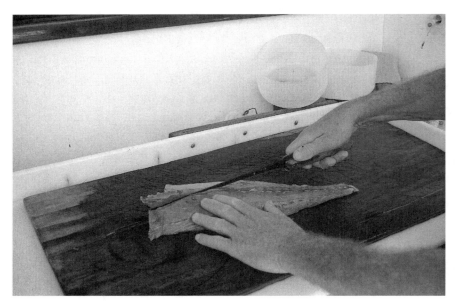

*A fresh-caught bluefish makes a fine bait that may be used whole, or filleted, as is being done here. Many anglers fish just a single fillet, although others prefer a pair of fillets rigged on a double-hook rig with a fluorescent orange plastic skirt.*

wire through the back of the bluefish and have it exit forward of the dorsal fin, near the head. This places the hook within a couple of inches of the tail. Then secure the leader wire to the eye of the head hook using a haywire twist.

If you're using a big bluefish as bait, you'll find that it's extremely active as it swims about attempting to free itself. To minimize its capacity to do so, cut off the tail fins—but don't cut off the tail so it bleeds. This will keep the bluefish attempting to swim and emitting distress signals, which often attracts sharks from a great distance. With the two-hook rig even a big shark taking a giant bite out of the bluefish is apt to get hooked.

With the second outfit, ease the bluefish in the water, pay out 125 feet of line, and attach your Snap Float. Stream the float out 75 feet and place the outfit in a rod holder.

Our first *Linda June* was ideally situated for setting one outfit in a rod holder at the stern, another amidship, and the third at the

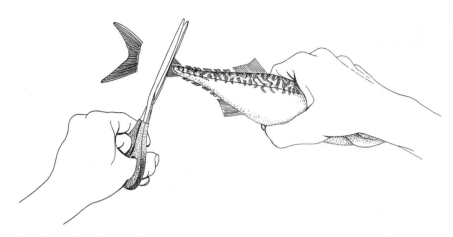

*To reduce a live bait's ability to swim effectively, use a pair of scissors and cut off its tail fins, taking care not to cut the meat. This technique works well with bluefish, yellowtail snappers, mackerel, and bonito, and results in the baitfish swimming about excitedly, emitting distress signals that attract any sharks in the area.*

bow. The boat's walkaround feature made access easy, and kept the outfits 12 feet apart.

Rig the third outfit's bait, run it down to a depth of 50 to 75 feet, place the Snap Float on the line, and permit it to drift out 40 or 50 feet from the boat. You might care to try a large whole squid

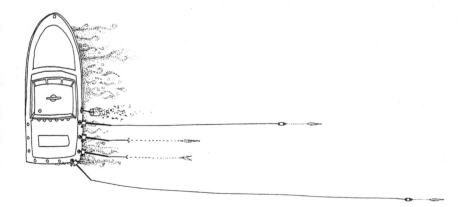

*The author usually fishes with three baits in the water, with a pitch bait held in reserve on board for sharks that approach on the surface. If you want to fish with all four baits in the water, keep one close astern so it can immediately be retrieved to pitch to a cruising shark.*

as bait; these are very plentiful on the offshore grounds and constitute a major portion of the diet of many pelagic sharks. I prefer to rig a 12- to 15-inch-long squid with a double hook, with the lead hook in the head of the squid and the trailing hook through the rear of the body near the tentacles. Rigged in this manner the squid takes on a lifelike appearance as it's drifted along, the tentacles fluttering enticingly on the drift.

Using this basic approach you'll have three baits at different depths in the water column where sharks may be cruising. They'll be at varying distances behind the boat, keeping them well separated, and the likelihood of a crossover is somewhat minimized with the outfits separated by 12-foot or longer intervals.

Make certain to bait up the fourth outfit, preferably without a sinker and using a fillet as bait, for you want a bait that is ready and easy to present to a shark that may show on the surface, having ignored the deep lines.

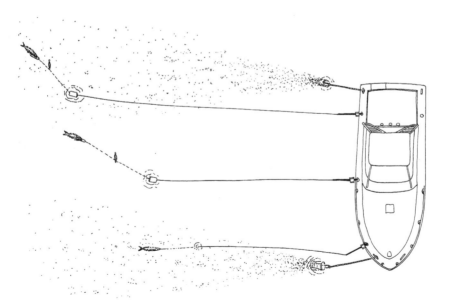

*This is the author's favorite chumming setup. A chum-dispensing bucket is set at the bow and another at the stern, with three baits in the water at different depths in the water column. A fourth outfit is baited and kept ready in the cockpit to use as a pitch bait for those occasions when a shark suddenly appears right at the boat, usually trying to eat the chum bucket!*

Toward this end, I know of several shark fishermen who don't even bother with putting a bait in the water, but wait until a shark appears on the surface or in their chum line before they go to work with a bait. While I prefer the three-baits-in-the-water system, with one in reserve for cruisers, the choice is up to you.

With the three baits in the water, and the automatic chum bucket doing its thing of oozing ground chum, it now becomes a waiting game, with the fourth outfit rigged and ready.

## Waiting for Strikes

With the big, colorful Snap Floats in clear view and spread out, it's important to be alert to their position. Normally they're in position and drifting along with the boat. There are times when a shark will pick up a bait and move off with it, swimming either toward the boat or off to the side, and this will quickly become apparent with the movement of the float being contrary to the normal drift. I liken this to a sunfish taking a worm bait in a farm pond and swimming off with it, yet never pulling the bobber beneath the surface. If you strike too soon, you may take the bait away from it. Far better with both the sunfish and the shark to hesitate and give it more time to mouth the bait, where the hook will be in a good position to penetrate.

Should the shark move toward the boat, as indicated by the float moving toward the boat, remove the rod and reel from the rod holder and reel up the slack so that as the line comes taut and the shark begins to move away, you're ready to strike.

I caution you to resist the temptation to immediately check the bait when you observe that there's been some activity. Sometimes, even despite a two-hook rig, a shark will mangle the bait and fail to get hooked. In all probability it won't have destroyed the entire bait, and if you simply permit it to drift along the shark will come back for a second bite, this time getting the hook well back in its jaw where it will be in a position to penetrate.

Quite often the shark will make a quick move, and with a taut line the Snap Float will snap free and slide on the line, at which time you should attempt to reel in until the line comes tight, all the time with your rod tip low and pointed in the direction the line is moving. Then move the drag lever to the strike position and with maximum force lift back smartly to set the hook, striking several times to ensure that the hook is firmly seated beyond the barb. If all goes well, just hold on and let that reel scream its banshee song as the shark begins its first run.

This is when it's important for the remainder of the cockpit crew not to fiddle-faddle. Move quickly to retrieve the two lines still in the water and avoid the potential of a tangle, which surely can happen, as there's no saying where the shark may be headed. Once aboard, place the outfits and their baits out of the way, preferably in rod holders other than those in the gunwales, so they're out of the way and the cockpit is clear for the angler to maneuver if need be.

## Fighting the Fish

There are two schools of thought as to what to do next. I've known many sharkers who prefer to fight their shark from a dead boat, as this maintains the chum line and maintains the status quo. This can be done with some sharks, and especially if you're using heavy tackle in the 50- or 80-pound class. If, however, you're using 30-pound-class outfits, as many of us prefer to do, you might be hard-pressed to stop, turn, and land a heavyweight shark from a dead boat.

It's also difficult to fight a shark from a dead boat in a rough sea or where there is a lot of surface chop. Should you choose to start up—almost essential for most sportfishermen, as the angler can't really go forward on the high decks—immediately try to position the boat so that the shark is off a stern quarter.

This enables you to easily move forward should the shark charge the boat, as often happens, which is when you want the ability to maneuver quickly to avoid a slack line. If you're using trolling rods and have a fighting chair, by all means let your angler settle into the chair, buckle up into the fighting harness, and position the footrest so he can go to work pumping the shark with minimum strain on arms and shoulders, using his legs for added support while pumping the gladiator up from the depths.

Should you choose to fight the fish standing up with a shoulder or kidney harness and fighting belt, then buckle up as soon as the shark is struck and move to a stern corner, where you can brace your thighs against the coaming padding. Most boats have sufficient freeboard that you can achieve a comfort level and some support. You might also consider a safety line of ¼-inch nylon line attached to your harness, which in turn should be looped onto a stern cleat. I'm always concerned about safety, and you should be too. You certainly don't want someone to lose his balance while strapped into a shoulder harness and gimbal fighting belt with a big shark on the end of the line.

No two big sharks are alike. Some, like the thresher and mako, will fight on the surface. The mako will often provide a display of aerial antics that shows off its brute strength, often leaping 15 feet or more into the air.

What you don't want to do is tighten down hard on a just-hooked shark in the hope of making a quick job of landing it. I've seen anglers do this with 80- and 130-pound-class outfits, and suddenly find themselves with 300 or 400 pounds of wild shark at the boat, whereupon the shark comes to the realization that it's hooked. Suddenly the gladiator unleashes all its strength, with a seesaw battle ensuing. If the shark crashes against the boat, a dangerous situation develops as the person handling the wire has loose wire and a wild shark within an arm length of the transom. Bad scene.

Instead, permit the shark to make several sustained runs. You can pretty much control the amount of line out by moderate maneuvering of the boat, kicking it into reverse gear if necessary to help the angler in the chair.

Toward this end, it's important to coach the angler if he's a newcomer to sportfishing for sharks. I've seen anglers struggle themselves to exhaustion because they didn't know how to pump a fish. The key is fishing a firm drag, lowering your rod tip and reeling on the downstroke, then firmly lifting back with the rod tip—while not reeling—and only retrieving line as you lower the rod tip. Develop a nice easy rhythm and don't try to turn the reel handle at all as a fish is taking line from the drag. This is a lost cause, and will cause you to lose circulation and strength in your arms.

## Wiring and Releasing or Keeping Sharks

As the shark is led to the boat, your cockpit crew should be extremely clear as to who is doing what. One person should be assigned to handle the leader wire, another to handle the flying gaff if the shark is to be retained, and the third person to handle a straight gaff and have the responsibility of using it to control and get a tail rope on the shark's tail so it can be secured.

Everybody should wear gloves of heavy-duty Australian leather, preferably wet gloves, as they provide a much better grip on both the wire leader and gaffs than do dry gloves. If the shark is to be released, you'll need only two people to assist, one handling the wire and the other cutting it. The same is true when tagging a shark prior to release.

Handling leader wire, especially 250-pound test or heavier, is serious business. Never, ever wrap wire around your hands or arms, as it can result in catastrophic injury. The key is making loops in the wire with a firm grasp, so that should it be necessary to let go you simply open your hand, and the loops fall free and away, without chance of any entanglement.

Toward this end it pays to practice wiring while ashore, having someone pretending to be a fish, and testing your mettle and dexterity in handling a wire with intense pressure on it. It's especially important, if not most important, to learn how to released coiled wire from your hand. I repeat, **never wrap the wire around your hands or arms.**

It's important that you maintain constant pressure as you grasp the leader. Yanking on it will often excite a shark and cause it to make another run. Firm and steady pressure is essential as you guide the shark within range of the gaff or release wire cutter.

The best gaff shot for a shark to be boated is in the gill area, as this is an easy entry for the gaff and gives you quick and immediate control of the head. You don't want to gaff a shark in the middle of the body, where the gaff becomes the fulcrum as the shark freely shakes its head and shoulders, all the while snapping viciously with its teeth.

*It's extremely dangerous to bring a shark aboard the boat, as is being done here. One slip and serious injury could result from the vicious jaws of a mako. The author strongly recommends tying the shark alongside, and always remembering that there's no such thing as a "dead shark." Many hours after being landed sharks have been known to inflict serious injury.*

As this is going on the angler, either standing behind the crew or still in the fighting chair, should be alert that at this moment anything can happen, including the shark ripping free of a poorly placed gaff, or literally becoming airborne at the side of the boat. As so often happens, the first shot with the gaff may miss, and the tremendous pressure placed on the wireman by the excited shark will often rip the wire from his hands. The shark may then take off on another run of 100 yards or more, perhaps even requiring another hour to bring back to the boat! It does happen.

If everything goes well in placing the first gaff, the straight gaff should quickly be placed in the shark's tail and a tail rope secured around the tail and drawn up tight so the shark can't slip off. With both the head secured with the flying gaff hook and rope, and the gaff handle removed, secure the rope to a stern cleat on one side of the boat, and then quickly secure the tail rope to a stern cleat on the other side.

If you want to secure the shark alongside as opposed to across the transom, draw the shark forward headfirst toward the bow, securing the flying gaff line to an amidships cleat and the tail rope to a stern cleat. Then, and only then, when you're certain the shark is secure, cut the leader with a pair of long-handled wire cutters.

I know that many anglers bring their sharks on board, and I guess it's a matter of personal choice. But having tangled with many species of sharks, in waters on all three coasts, I'm a firm believer in keeping them lashed rather than bringing them aboard. A good mind-set is to feel that a shark never, ever dies. I've seen sharks unloaded at dockside eight hours after they were caught with their jaws still snapping wildly. Indeed, each season sees many bystanders injured at dockside by "dead" sharks. Sharks are dangerous, and I can't stress enough the importance of always treating them as being alive and vicious, even—or I should say *especially*—when they're on the dock.

In the event you plan on releasing a shark, I recommend that you cut the wire as near to the shark as it may safely be accomplished. By far the best tool is a pair of long-handled—24 to 36 inches long—wire cutters, such as those used while working with barbed wire.

I would never recommend using a pair of ordinary wire-cutting pliers and attempting to cut the leader within a couple of feet of the snapping jaws of a vicious shark. Frankly, it's just irresponsible to do so, as sharks are so fast that in an instant you could incur serious, life-threatening injury. If regular pliers are all that you have on board, make the wire cut from a safe distance.

I've seen de-hookers designed to remove the hook from the jaw of a shark when it's brought alongside, and I don't dispute that they work. They may be especially effective when used by professional crewmen who are handling sharks daily, but for the recreational fisherman who may only land a couple of sharks per season, I recommend against using a de-hooker. It's just too dangerous getting hands and fingers too near a shark's jaw, regardless of the species or its size.

I've been aboard when sharks that had previously been hooked were brought alongside and had as many as two hooks in them. Observation disclosed that the sharks were none the worse as a result of the hooks, which appeared well rusted and no doubt soon rusted fully away and fell out.

## CATCHING CRUISING SHARKS

It's important to stress that you should always be alert to the water surrounding the boat, all 360 degrees. I always like to have a lookout on the bridge, as often sharks will appear where you least expect them. All too often the crew in the cockpit are concentrating their attention in the direction that the lines are trailing as you drift along, not realizing that a shark may be circling on the other side of the boat.

When you do spot a shark on the surface, or cruising beneath the hull, don't fret over trying to retrieve the three baits that are in the water. That's why you've got a backup outfit rigged, baited, and ready. A technique that I've often found effective is to use a "pitch bait" approach in presenting the bait to the cruising shark.

Place the rod and reel in a rod holder, and strip off 50 feet of line onto the deck. Then grasp the bait and move to a position on the boat where you can anticipate where the shark will be swimming. Once you feel it's within range, use an underhand pitch, much like that used in fast-pitch softball, which will arch the bait into the air, line trailing from the deck, so that it splashes in ahead of the cruising shark and in its range of vision.

Then grasp the line and, if necessary, begin a hand-over-hand retrieve to keep the bait fluttering and in the range of the shark's vision. The fillet bait is especially effective, as its flat surface and nominal weight tend to keep it buoyant if there's a light drift. Often a shark will swim right up to the bait and engulf it in one fell swoop. This is why I like to have control of the line by lightly holding it and permitting it to pay out off the deck until it comes taut to the rod in the rod holder, or to the angler who by now should have the rod out of the holder. Then as the shark continues to swim off, with line paying off the reel in free spool and the rod pointed in the direction the line is moving, lock up the reel to strike drag and lift back smartly to set the hook.

Don't hesitate to strike two or three times, as you want the hook to penetrate in past the barb. Too lightly set a drag or too light a striking motion in my view will often cause the hook to only partially penetrate the shark. After a long run the hook will simply fall out, never having fully penetrated beyond the barb in the first place.

*Live bonito, tuna, mackerel, sardines, and other forage are excellent for attracting strikes from sharks searching for a meal. Use a rigging needle to run a piece of rigging twine through the bait's eye sockets and tie it to the bend of the hook. This permits the bait to swim unimpeded when either drifted or slowly trolled.*

Years ago, before the advent of the automatic-chum-bucket approach described earlier, I often used a mesh bag filled with chum to accomplish the same purpose, simply dispensing chum without my having to tend the chum bucket. On numerous occasions I had sharks leisurely swim up, grab the chum bag, and literally shake it, and themselves, until they eventually ripped it from the line. I've even had big sharks attack the chum bucket, as the scent of the chum oozing from the bucket drives them into a frenzy to get at the source.

With respect to live decoys, veteran sharkers know that a live baitfish will emit distress signals that carry for a great distance—and that the shark's keen senses will immediately home in on the source of the distress. As such they'll run a rigging needle and piece of rigging twine through the eye sockets of a mackerel, bluefish, yellowtail snapper, blue runner, or other fish, tie one end securely to the fish, and make a loop onto the other end of the twine.

On reaching the fishing grounds, the outriggers are lowered. Then the rigging twine with a live baitfish is secured to an outrigger line and its length adjusted so the baitfish can swim unimpeded 2 or 3 feet beneath the surface. It will often swim about excitedly, occasionally being lifted clear of the water as the boat rocks, where it will provide a surface disturbance.

This combination of a live decoy swimming close at hand from the outriggers, sending out distress signals, and the potent chum drifting from the chum bucket in a constant stream, is guaranteed to attract any sharks in the area.

I've observed many occasions when a shark is attracted by the live bait decoy, leisurely swimming up to investigate. As soon as the shark approaches, the outrigger line is retrieved and a live baitfish with a hook in it quickly drifted out or repositioned into the outrigger to tease the shark into striking.

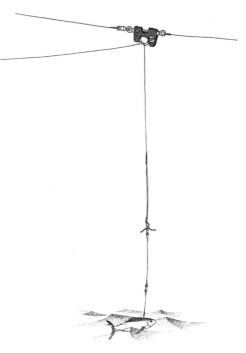

*A live baitfish, suspended from the clip of an outrigger so it's right at the surface, swims about excitedly and transmits distress signals to cruising sharks.*

In Bermuda many years ago Pete Perinchief and I often fished Challenger and Argus Banks, anchoring up and chumming for yellowfin tuna and the occasional wahoo and dolphin that moved into the chum line. For sharks we employed a live yellowtail snapper, blue runner, or jack crevalle that was caught on a light spinning outfit and tiny piece of bait.

In those days we simply placed the hook through the back of the yellowtail, just forward of the dorsal fin. We then flew a fishing kite off the stern, carried in the direction the wind wanted to take it, so it was a couple of hundred feet from the boat. Our fishing line was attached to an outrigger clip on the kite line and streamed out, with the line length adjusted so that the live bait swam excitedly right on the surface, often being lifted into the air as a gust of wind pushed the kite higher.

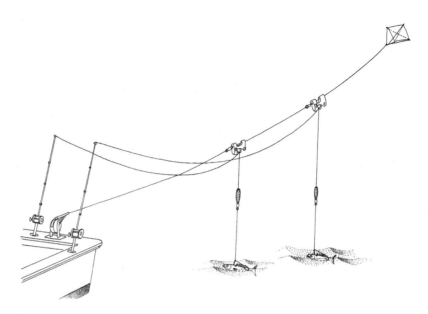

*A fishing kite is very effective to fish a pair of live baitfish on the surface. The lines are set so the baits are struggling on the surface, emitting distress signals to cruising sharks. As a shark takes the bait, the line is snapped free from an outrigger clip attached to the kite line.*

The excited antics of the yellowtail, and its distress signals, prompted responses from gigantic hammerhead sharks, plus equally huge bull sharks, and even enticed strikes from dolphin and wahoo that investigated the commotion.

## NIGHT FISHING

The majority of sharkers do their fishing during hours of daylight, but by far the best, most consistent shark fishing I've enjoyed has been after dark, particularly when seeking albacore, yellowfin, bluefin, and bigeye tuna in the offshore canyons while fishing along the edge of the continental shelf. Often big mako, thresher, tiger, and blue sharks would leisurely swim into the chum line intended for tuna, their huge bulk clearly visible under the *Linda June's* quartz lights. Almost without exception these fish would respond to a slab of fillet cut from just about any fish that was available, the bloodier the better.

*If you're planning an extended stay overnight on the offshore shark grounds, make certain you've got ample chum and bait on board. A couple of containers of ground chum, a couple of flats of mackerel or menhaden, and a supply of whole squid and butterfish is included aboard the* Linda June *whenever the author heads offshore.*

Indeed, night fishing for sharks is the rule among some dedicated shark buffs. In the deep waters off the edge of the continental shelf the two periods that the pelagic sharks seem most active are shortly after dusk and around daybreak, which seems to parallel the feeding patterns and activity of many species of fish.

To enhance the opportunity of scoring with deep-drifting baits at night, many anglers add a Cyalume light stick to their leader. Snapping the light stick activates it, creating a chemical reaction that results in its emitting an eerie glow in the dark depths. The light sticks are available in red, blue, and green, with green being the most popular among shark, broadbill swordfish, and tuna fishermen. The illumination in the depths, the scent of chum, and the smell of a hook bait or distress signals transmitted by a live bait all combine to bring sharks within range of a hook bait.

## ANCHORING

While drifting and chumming is the preferred method of most off-shore shark fishermen, there are times when it pays to anchor over prime locations such as along the edge of a canyon wall where there is an upwelling of ocean currents, or adjacent to an underwater ledge or wrecks. Spots like this often have an abundance of forage, such as bottom feeders that congregate on the ledges and around the wrecks. Sharks know there is an easy meal in the offing and regularly frequent the areas.

Attempting to drift over the area doesn't usually prove effective; the speed of the drift moves you along too quickly. It then becomes beneficial to use your loran or GPS coordinates in conjunction with your fishfinder to locate the exact spot where you feel the sharks will be located. Then drop a marker buoy and, while taking into account wind direction and tidal current drift, position your anchor to bring you in close proximity to the desired spot.

Once settled in, commence chumming operations much as though you were drifting, including the placement of lines. Often it becomes a waiting game. While a pair of lines may be drifted back to the structure, as described earlier, I also like to work a line when I'm anchored up. Fish the outfit in a rod holder, and pull off 150 to 200 feet of line, permitting it to drift back in the chum line naturally.

Once the bait has drifted 200 feet from the boat, pull it back in hand over hand, depositing it in a round 20- or 30-gallon trash can. This keeps the line from becoming tangled on the deck or, worse still, wrapping around an ankle. Then pay out the bait again. It's a tedious process, but the free-drifting bait settling with the chum toward the wreck or ledge will often bring strikes.

On occasion before we anchor we like to bottom fish for snapper or grouper on southern wrecks, or ling, whiting, small codfish, or pollack on northern wrecks. All of these make excellent live baits, and which is why the sharks are congregating in the area in the first place.

In this type of anchored fishing it's wise to have your anchor release system rigged and ready at the helm station on the bridge, so you can instantly start up the engines when a shark is hooked, and immediately be free of the anchor, returning later to pick up the anchor rope and its marker buoy.

Once off the anchor rope, proceed with fighting the shark much as though you hooked it while drifting, always keeping alert to the fact that the anchor line and buoy are out there somewhere. Do everything possible to maneuver the shark away from becoming entangled in them, which can result in one awful mess.

## PINPOINTING SHARKS

One thing you should always be alert to is that sharks travel with their food source. While you may experience excellent shark fishing in an area early in the season, don't make the mistake of thinking that sharks will be in the same area throughout the entire season.

*Shark fishing is often a waiting game, requiring a great deal of patience. Once you've baited up with a fresh bluefish fillet on a double-hook rig with a fluorescent orange plastic skirt, it's just a matter of adjusting a Snap Float for the depth at which you want the bait suspended, permitting it to drift 100 feet from the boat, and waiting until a hungry shark moves into the slick to take the bait.*

John Raguso, one of Long Island's excellent charter skippers and a renowned boating and sportfishing authority, sails his *MarCeeJay* from Shinnecock. His first forays offshore are often 60 or 70 miles seaward, where migrating schools of bluefish are located, with some moving in from offshore and others migrating from the south. Big mako sharks, thresher sharks, and lots of blue sharks are close at hand, and the fishing is often extraordinary as he drifts his anglers along the canyon edges and the 100-fathom line.

Many shark anglers fail to realize that bluefish and other forage are just passing through, and when the bluefish move inshore you've got to adjust accordingly. It then often becomes a matter of setting up your drift just 20 or 30 miles offshore to take advantage of the grounds where the bluefish have set up summer residence. John carefully watches the movements of the schools of bluefish and especially of the school bluefin tuna that migrate during June, planning his shark excursions accordingly.

Among some of the spots John likes during the summer months are the wrecks of the *Arundo, Lillian, Stolt Dagali, Pinta, Three Sisters, G & D, Yankee, Good, Gunboat, San Diego, Linda,* and *Oregon,* all of which are marked on geodetic charts or local fishing charts. Many of these spots are located in 20 or 30 fathoms of water and save him the long run to the canyons and 100-fathom line. Importantly, the bluefish take up residence around these wrecks because they feature an abundance of herring and sand eels high in the water column as well as a multitude of ling and other bottom feeders. The sharks know this and are always close at hand. As a bonus the variety is expanded by the tiger sharks and hammerhead sharks that tend to arrive when the waters warm.

As noted earlier, you can drift these wreck areas leisurely. If the wind is moving you along too quickly, however, don't hesitate to drop anchor to position yourself adjacent to the wreck to set up your chum slick.

Newcomers to shark fishing have often asked me what I consider the most important items to be successful at catching these fine game fish. While tackle, equipment, and boats in sterling condition are all prime requisites, my response has always been that being alert on the fishing grounds and paying attention to detail is what makes for successful sharking.

While drifting along and paying out a chum line, be ever alert to what's happening around you. It'll often make the difference between tangling with a tough-fighting predator and experiencing an uneventful day.

*The author's wife, June, sits comfortably in a bucket harness as she battles a huge hammerhead shark hooked on a trolled mullet bait while fishing at the tip of the Tongue of the Ocean off Chub Cay in the Bahamas. The key in getting a big shark to take a surface-trolled bait is to troll slowly, and bring the bait within its range of vision.*

# 8

# Trolling

Offshore trolling is generally most productive for marlin, wahoo, dolphin, and members of the tuna clan. For the most part sharks are an incidental trolling catch as they crash trolled lures or natural baits intended for other game fish. There are exceptions to the rule, however, and many shark anglers have developed specific trolling techniques that prove extremely effective. This is particularly true when large migrations of sharks follow the migration paths of tuna, mackerel, bonito, and other schooling forage species.

The trolling concept centers on the old adage that "where you find the food you'll find the sharks." I vividly recall an exciting day's trolling off San Diego, while fishing aboard the *Angela*. Our target was striped marlin, and we'd trolled unsuccessfully for a couple of hours, all the while looking for birds, which would disclose the presence of sardine schools; the billfish were sure to be close at hand.

Suddenly, almost as though they were scheduled for an appearance, the sky was alive with screaming and diving gulls, while the surface was awash with frightened sardines, in tightly packed schools, leaping into the air en masse as they sought to escape the predators below.

Fortunately we had several live mackerel in the live well, which we streamed astern as we circled the school. In less time than it takes to tell, a huge striped marlin crashed the lively mackerel, and I had my work cut out for me. The boat did not have a fighting chair, and I was obliged to go toe-to-toe with the striper while standing up with a rod belt. The acrobat was in the air more than the water. Eventually it tired and I got it alongside.

In the excitement of catching the marlin, the other mackerel bait had expired. Reeling it aboard, we rigged it ahead of a plastic-skirted trolling head, and streamed it astern in the hope of a repeat performance with a striped marlin.

We again began to circle the excited sardines, when the distinctive fin of a mako appeared, lazily swimming perhaps 20 feet from the thousands of sardines. You might think the shark would be charging into the baitfish, but instead it just swam along, perhaps waiting for a sick or injured sardine to lag behind, making for an easy meal.

Instead, as we eased back on the throttle and circled tight to the school, the erratic action of the spoon-shaped trolling head and its undulating plastic skirt caused the trailing mackerel bait to swim enticingly, perhaps appearing as a wounded baitfish.

The moment the bait was within its range of vision, the mako charged without hesitation, crashing the mackerel with mouth agape, and boiling the surface white as it felt the hook sink home.

Typical of most makos, it provided a near-surface fight, completely clearing the water on two occasions. Unlike marlin, which leap, thrash, twist, and tail-walk, the mako exits the water much like a missile, sort of cartwheels through the air, and then crashes back in. At boatside this particular mako looked to weigh about 75 pounds, typical of most California makos, and was promptly released.

On this day we were opportunists and capitalized on the surface action with the schooling sardines, where we sighted the shark before presenting a trolled bait to it.

Such is not always the case. Each June off the Jersey coast we experience a migration run of both medium and giant bluefin tuna, as they move north to summer off New England and Canada's Maritime provinces. The tuna feed on migrating bluefish and mackerel, both of which are traveling in huge schools to their summer range.

For years I fished for the bluefins, and the favorite technique was to employ a Reel Seat Spreader Bar rigged with anywhere from five to nine whole Atlantic mackerel. Four mackerel would be rigged with their mouths tied shut and attached to the arm of the spreader; occasionally a second mackerel was rigged behind the first, for a total of eight. The last mackerel would be rigged with a 10/0 or 12/0 Martu hook in it, and trail the mackerel by a foot or so.

As the spreader bar rigged with mackerel was slowly trolled at a speed that kept it fluttering on the surface, it made an attractive appearance in the water, simulating a small patch of mackerel excitedly jumping about, with a lone mackerel trailing the pack. It was this lone mackerel that would invariably be struck by the tuna, most of which were in the 100- to 125-pound class.

Mako and thresher sharks often played havoc with meticulously rigged mackerel baits of the fleet that trolled for tuna in the *Bacardi* wreck area just inshore of Hudson Canyon. We fished the area often with our *Linda June* and on a daily basis the radio chatter would include someone cussing the sharks, which often blindly assaulted a spreader bar rig, ripping several mackerel from it and completely missing the trailing mackerel with a hook in it.

I suspect the tuna would see the trailing mackerel and consider it the one most easily captured, whereas the sharks would home in on the scent of five to nine mackerel thrashing about and just charge in, mouths wide open to engulf all they could. I must admit, there were occasions when the tuna played hard to get, and it was a welcome change of pace to see an explosion in the wake and hook up to an angry mako, thresher, or blue shark.

*Most offshore trollers troll at a fast speed when seek-ing tuna and billfish. When sharks are encountered in an area, it's best to switch to a slow troll and bring the baits within range of the shark. Often sharks will sound at the approach of a boat, at which time taking your engines out of gear and permitting the baits to settle will often result in a pickup.*

It's interesting to note that for several consecutive seasons our biggest bluefish of the entire season were caught on the spreader bar rigs while we were targeting tuna and sharks. This reinforced the theory that bluefish were in the area, usually providing a meal for the tuna and sharks, but the bluefish had to eat too, and would assault the small-er mackerel that were also migrating.

## TROLLING TECHNIQUES

While chumming sharks is unquestionably the most popular technique on all three coasts, there is a select group of shark-ers who prefer trolling. The trolling fraternity likes to keep moving, and probing the waters for their quarry. They some-times cruise until gull activity and its accompanying bait are located, after which they set out their trolling spread or simply blind troll over struc-ture or areas known to regularly have a population of sharks in residence.

When I'm targeting sharks I usually troll with just two outfits, as opposed to six or eight outfits when seeking tuna or marlin. For the majority of trolling encounters with sharks, regulation 50-pound-class big-game outfits work nicely. Trollers generally prefer conventional trolling rods measuring 6 feet, 6 inches, to 7 feet in overall length; this length keeps the line higher in the air, and makes for ease in keeping the trolled baits or lures near the surface. Throw-lever reels should be loaded with 50- or 80-pound-test line.

Stand-up rods, generally 12 to 18 inches shorter than conventional trolling rods, may also be used, especially if you're fishing from a small boat that doesn't have a fighting chair in the cockpit.

## Terminal Tackle

I like to double the last 12 feet of the terminal end of the line, using either a Bimini knot or a surgeon's loop. I then tie on a 250-pound-test Sampo ball–bearing swivel with a coastlock snap using an offshore swivel knot. While a swivel of this test isn't really necessary, its larger size lends itself to ease in handling. When you reach out with a gloved hand to wire the shark alongside, the swivel's size gives you a better hand-hold. The double line also enables you to exert extra drag pressure on the shark as it's brought close to the boat, where it will either be gaffed or released, also giving you better control.

### BIMINI TWIST

The strongest loop knot of all — but also the most difficult to tie — the Bimini Twist is used to create double line for pursuing strong saltwater fish with relatively light line. These directions are for creating a double line of five feet or less. Two people may be required for anything longer. You will need to practice this knot a lot to get it right.

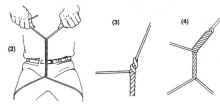

(1) Measure a loop slightly more than twice the footage you want for the double line. Holding the standing line and tag end together, twist the loop about 20 times.

(2) Sit down and put your legs into the loop and apply outward pressure. At the same time, pull out on the standing line and tag ends to force the twists tightly together.
(3) Maintaining leg pressure, hold the standing line in one hand with the tension slightly off vertical. With the other hand, move the tag end to a right angle from the twists and gradually gain tension. The tag line should begin to roll over the twists.
(4) Continue outward leg pressure on the loop. Steer the tag end into a tight downward spiral over the twists.
(5) Continue to maintain leg pressure once the tag end reaches the bottom of the twists. With the hand that has been holding the standing line, place index finger in crotch of line where loop joins knot to prevent slippage of last turn. Take a half-hitch with tag end around one strand of the loop and pull it tight.

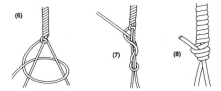

(6) With the half-hitch holding the knot, you can release leg pressure, but keep the loop stretched out. With the remaining tag end, take a half-hitch around both strands of the loop, but do not pull tight.
(7) Take two more turns around both strands of the loop, winding inside the bend of the line formed by the loose half-hitch and toward the main knot. Put the tag end through the bend of the loose half-hitch created in step 6.
(8) Pull the tag end to gather and tighten the loops around the main knot. Trim the tag end.

## OFFSHORE SWIVEL KNOT

1. Slip loop end of double-line leader through eye of swivel. Rotate loop end a half-turn to put a single twist between loop and swivel eye.

2. Pass the loop with the twist over the swivel. Hold end of the loop, plus both legs of the double-line leader with one hand. Let swivel slide to other end of double loops now formed.

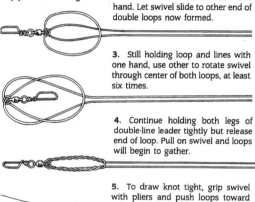

3. Still holding loop and lines with one hand, use other to rotate swivel through center of both loops, at least six times.

4. Continue holding both legs of double-line leader tightly but release end of loop. Pull on swivel and loops will begin to gather.

5. To draw knot tight, grip swivel with pliers and push loops toward eye with fingers, while still keeping standing lines of the leader pulled tight.

You've got a choice between stainless-steel cable and stainless-steel solid wire for leader material. An all-around favorite is cable or wire testing out with a breaking strength of 250 pounds. The cable has a slight edge insofar as shark fishermen are concerned, because it's more flexible than wire and does not have the drawback of kinking. Sharks are notorious for wrapping themselves in the leader as they twist and turn, especially blue sharks and spinners. This will occasionally cause a wrap or kink in the wire, which will cause it to break when pressure is brought to bear.

Make certain you use a top-quality crimping tool when making up cable leaders. I'll often use a pair of crimps to ensure a solid connection. With single-strand stainless-steel leader wire it's easy to make solid connections using a haywire twist.

I prefer using 10- to 12-foot-long leaders. Midway I place a single 250-pound-test Sampo ball-bearing swivel. In this way the wireman can grasp the first swivel as the double line gets on the reel, then reach out and grasp the second swivel relatively easily, getting a firm handhold as the shark gets alongside the boat. This second swivel isn't absolutely essential, but I've found it effective on leaders while chumming or trolling.

## Lures

There are literally dozens of trolling lures that can be used, either singly or in combination with a natural bait, when trolling for sharks. I prefer a lure that tracks straight yet pushes water and stays on the surface, especially when I trail a rigged bait within the skirt. Toward this end, there's no question that a rigged bait, because of the scent it emits, will receive more strikes than a plain trolling lure, regardless of its action.

With the trolling head and skirt placed on the leader, use a pair of crimps to secure a 10/0 or 12/0 Martu or any of the forged big-game hooks manufactured by Mustad, Eagle Claw, Owner, or Gamakatsu. The state-of-the-art hooks available today, with laser-sharpened points and chemically treated metal, are far superior to what was available just a few years ago.

## Baits

By far the best forage species to rig on the hook is whatever species predominates in the area, although almost any fish works out fine. I've used several different species of mackerel, bonito, little tunny, mullet, and bluefish while trolling and pitch-baiting, and the sharks will devour them all. The key is matching the size of the bait to the hook. A big bait may necessitate rigging a second or trailing hook onto the leader, positioned 8 to 12 inches behind the first one. The latter ensures a hookup when the shark crashes a bait from the side, often biting through the middle of the bait, where the stinger hook catches it.

A very effective way of rigging the bait on the hook is to insert it into the mouth, then exit it in the baitfish's stomach just behind the pectoral fins. You can then run a rigging needle and rigging twine through the lower jaw of the bait, through the hook's ringed eye, and exit through the top of the jaw. Then tie the twine securely, which will hold the hook in place.

With larger baitfish some anglers will use a 4- to 6-inch piece of heavy single-strand stainless-steel leader wire between the hook and the primary leader. When this short trace is used, you insert the

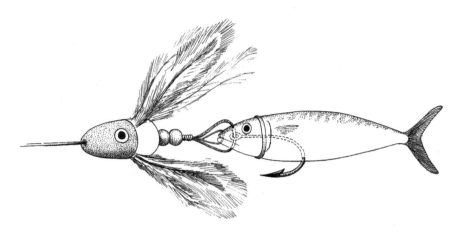

*Rigged in this manner, a whole baitfish is trolled with ease, fluttering on the surface and literally swimming beneath the surface as it is slowly trolled. Many shark fishermen add a feather skirt ahead of the bait, feeling that it enhances the shark-attracting effectiveness of the bait.*

hook through the bait's mouth, out the gill, and then insert it back in the gill and exit through the stomach, which places the hook well back in the bait. The rigging needle and twine are then inserted in the lower jaw of the bait, through the front-end loop of the short wire leader where it meets the primary leader, and out the upper jaw, where the twine is tied, securing the head.

A whole freshly caught bait will hold up very well for quite a while as you slowly troll an area frequented by sharks. While the whole baitfish make a nice bait that doesn't require much attention, I've also had excellent results when using a large strip bait, especially one cut from a little tunny, popularly called bonito throughout the South.

Little tunny have meat the color of beef, and they're a very long-lasting bait when cut from a fresh fish. The best baits are cut from the silvery underside of the fish. Make a cut so the bait is approximately ½ inch thick, and give it a torpedo shape, tapering toward the tail. Try to cut a 15- to 20-inch-long bait, which is ideal. The bait will have one side with the skin and the other of the exposed meat. As it's trolled along, many theorize that the bait gives off more scent because of the exposed meat than does a whole fish.

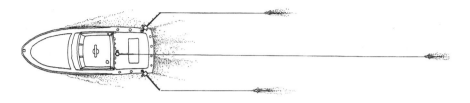

*The author usually trolls with just two baits in the water when seeking sharks. An option is a third line down the middle, set back 125 to 150 feet astern.*

Here too, it pays to rig the hook on a short 4- to 6-inch-long piece of 250-pound-test stainless-steel leader wire. Place the hook through the center of the strip bait and use rigging twine to secure the head of the bait to the short wire leader's loop where it meets the primary leader. You can also fabricate a safety pin snap into the short leader as you're making it, and use it to secure the head of the strip bait.

## FISHING BAITS

When trolling with either a whole baitfish or a strip bait, you should make certain not to troll at too fast a speed. I've found a lazy 3- or 4-knot trolling speed far more effective than the higher 6- or 7-knot speed customarily used for marlin and tuna with high-speed trolling lures.

The lazy troll and tantalizing bait that is emitting a scent enable a shark to home in on the bait.

I generally fish the baits dropped back from the outrigger about 100 to 125 feet behind the boat. This gets the baits off to the side of the nominal wake being churned up by a slow troll. Often you'll see the shark as it moves in on the bait. When it crashes the bait it'll pull the line from the outrigger clip, and several feet of slack line will settle before the line again becomes tight to the shark.

As the shark crashes the bait, it's intent on eating what it feels is a fish in distress. Its menacing set of dentures will slash the bait in an instant, with the viselike grip of its teeth locked onto the bait and, hopefully, the hook within its jaw.

It's important that you not have the drag set too tightly with the rod in the rod holder. I have the drags on my Penn International 30 VSW set just off from strike drag, so there is minimal pressure as the line comes tight. This enables me to effortlessly remove the rod and reel from the rod holder, then move the drag forward to strike position and, with the line taut, lift back firmly to set the hook.

All too often I've observed anglers who had their drags set much too tight while trolling for sharks—and for tuna and marlin as well, for that matter. With a tightly set drag and a shark screaming line from the reel, it becomes virtually impossible for even the strongest angler to remove the rod and reel from the rod holder. In the excitement of attempting to remove the outfit, I've observed many anglers inadvertently back off too far with the drag lever, throwing the reel into free spool. This results in no pressure on the line. With a fast fish taking line from the reel, the spool tends to overrun, causing a horrible backlash. It takes but an instant for the backlashed line to bind, not permitting line to flow from the reel and resulting in an immediate line break. Attention to detail is a critical part of shark fishing, and almost any big-game fishing. Just a little thing like an incorrect drag setting can make the difference between success and failure.

Once a shark has been hooked, you can ease back on the throttle somewhat, but shouldn't immediately put the boat in neutral. The slow forward movement of the boat will help keep the line tight to ensure that the hook is well seated in the shark's jaw. Don't worry about ripping the hook out, as sharks have extremely tough jaw tissue; once the hook is seated it usually stays put. Once the rod-and-reel outfit has been removed from the rod holder, and the angler seated in the fighting chair or buckled to the shoulder harness with the rod butt in the belt gimbal, then it's time to take the boat out of gear and settle down for the ensuing battle.

Care should be taken to keep the shark off a stern quarter if the angler is seated in a fighting chair or fighting the fish standing up in the cockpit. I don't rush a shark when it's first hooked. All too often

I've observed anglers who put tremendous initial pressure on a shark. The initial reaction of the shark is sometimes confusing. While you'd expect it would be wildly attempting to gain its freedom, there are times when they hardly react to being hooked.

If you put excessive initial pressure on the shark, you may well get it to boatside quickly—only to have it explode in a vicious rage with unbelievable strength and endurance, for it will not have expended any energy. In my view it's downright dangerous even trying to handle a wire leader and release a still-green shark at boatside. Far better to let the shark do its fighting

*Properly adjusted, a kidney harness and fighting belt make it relatively easy to fight a big shark on 30-pound-class stand-up tackle. The key in landing a big shark while trolling is to get the boat out of gear and position it so the angler is in a stern quarter, where the boat can lend assistance if it appears as though the shark will spool the angler.*

well away from the boat. Once it begins to tire, then bring pressure to bear to lead it alongside for either gaffing or release.

Those who shark fish from small boats, especially outboard boats, center consoles, and walkaround cabin models, find they prefer having their angler move to the bow of the boat. They find it easier maneuvering the boat and following the shark during the battle, as opposed to having to back down, where in a heavy sea you'll take water over the transom. We frequently did this on our first *Linda June,* where it was rather easy for the angler to move from the stern along the walkaround deck with its high rail, and even to sit down on the bow seat as we fought a big shark or other game fish.

Under no circumstances should an angler stand on the bow of any boat, especially some of the newer macho convertible boats that have no bow rail, while fighting any fish. One slip and an angler can easily fall overboard, an especially dangerous situation while wearing a shoulder harness and rod belt and attached to a heavy outfit with a wild shark on the end of the line.

## SPREADER RIGS

The spreader bar rig has grown in popularity among shark anglers, for as it's trolled on the surface it resembles a group of frightened and excited baitfish. For years I've used Reel Seat Spreader Bars, developed by Grant Toman and Dave Arbeitman, owners of the Reel Seat tackle shop in Brielle, New Jersey. Grant and Dave fabricate their bars from titanium, which has no memory, and its springiness results in baits trolled from the bars swimming with an enticing, lifelike action.

I've used a wide variety of natural baits on spreader bars, including several species of mackerel, mullet, sardines, balao, and whole squid. Using fresh baitfish is important with spreader bars, as soft baits or those that have been frozen for a long period of time will wash out quickly when trolled.

A prerequisite for using spreader bars while trolling is having the patience to rig the baits. You've got to rig anywhere from five to nine baits, which means sewing the lips closed and tying a harness around the head and gill covers. The individual fish are then either tied or snapped directly to the bar.

The individual trailing fish is rigged in much the same manner as described earlier when you troll with but a single bait. While the hope is always that the shark will take the trailing bait, I've had times when they slash in unmercifully and completely mangle the entire spread, literally holding on until they rip a couple of baits from the rig. It's mind-boggling the mess a shark can make of a neatly tied spreader bar of nine baits in just a single split-second onslaught of the rig! One, I might add, that may have taken half an hour or more to rig.

## DEEP TROLLING

Both of the trolling methods just described are for surface trolling the bait. Deep trolling is also effective with a single whole baitfish or a daisy chain of four of five baits rigged 12 to 18 inches apart. To rig a daisy chain I place a single crimp on the cable leader at each point I want to position a bait. I then tie shut the mouth of the bait, usually a mackerel, and also place a harness around its head and gills. I leave enough rigging twine to secure the bait to the cable leader just forward of the crimp, which prevents the bait from sliding down on the leader.

I repeat this procedure with each of the baits that form the daisy chain, rigging the trailing bait with the hook in it much the same as described earlier for surface trolling.

Both a single bait and the daisy chain can be sent into the depths with a downrigger. You've got to troll very slowly when fishing natural baits in the depths, for there's a lot of pressure brought to bear against the entire rig.

Downriggers are especially useful when you're trolling an area unsuccessfully, yet you continue to read concentrations of baitfish—sometimes huge schools that light up the color fishfinder—down 50 to 75 feet. When the bait is deep you won't see any surface action or bird play, and the area will appear sterile. Rest assured that the sharks are down where the bait is schooled up, and by employing a downrigger you'll be getting your baits down into the strike zone.

## LIVE BAITS

Live baits are also very effective when trolling for sharks. On the offshore grounds you're often able to use small trolling feathers and catch little tunny, Atlantic or Pacific bonito, and mackerel, all of which are excellent live baits.

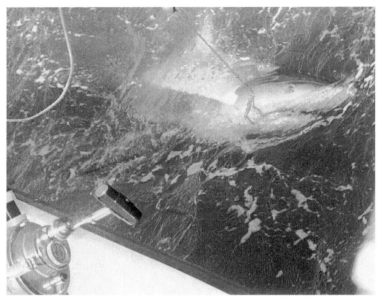

*This 8-foot-long bull shark crashed a mullet bait and gave the 50-pound outfit it was hooked on and Neal Yomans quite a workout. It was hooked off Jekyll Island, Georgia, an area frequented by many of the Atlantic's larger sharks that receives but minimal fishing pressure.*

They're easily rigged by running a rigging needle through the eye sockets, tying the rigging twine securely to the fish, and in turn tying it to the J part of a 10/0 or 12/0 hook. Hooked in this manner the live bait will actively swim about as it's trolled just beneath the surface. It's best to adjust your throttles to a speed that enables the fish to swim along unimpeded. You don't want to have it dragging across the surface, which will happen if the throttles are too far advanced.

Live baits are especially effective because they emit sound waves that are intercepted by roving sharks, which home in on the distress calls of forage species. Sharks much prefer to stalk a distressed fish—culling the herd, so to speak—as it's much easier for them to disable and feed on a fish that can't keep up with the school than it is to attack a healthy specimen.

## SURFACE FISH

Often while trolling you'll spot sharks sunning themselves on the surface, oblivious to anything around them. I've frequently almost trolled right over them in the frustration of trying to present a bait to them, all the while they completely ignored my best offerings, often moving away leisurely but continuing to stay on the surface.

One of the most successful techniques I've used when this situation develops is to reel in either a dead trolling bait or (preferably) a live one. I place the rod in the rod holder, strip 40 or 50 feet of line from the reel, and lay it loosely in the cockpit.

We then approach the shark at a very slow idle speed, taking the boat out of gear when we're within pitching distance of the shark. Standing in the cockpit, the leader is grasped and the bait is swung in a circular motion, then pitched underhanded at the shark. It's surprising how easy it is to pitch a bait 30 or even 50 feet.

If it's a live bait and drops in within 10 feet of the shark, you'll almost always arouse its interest. Sometimes the shark will charge it and engulf it in an instant. I've seen other times when the shark will leisurely circle the struggling baitfish, with the bonito or little tunny leaping clear of the water as it anticipates its fate. With one fleeting movement of its tail, the shark will zero it on its dinner, and you'll be hooked up. While this method usually works remarkably well, I've observed sharks that were completely disinterested, perhaps having filled their stomachs earlier!

## CHUMMING

Shark trollers are an innovative bunch, and I've known several who employed a chumming technique while trolling. They begin by using a hole cutter with an electric drill to cut a series of 1-inch-diameter holes in a 5-gallon plastic bucket. The bucket is then filled with frozen ground menhaden, mackerel, or herring chum. The lid is secured to the bucket, and a piece of ¼-inch rope is tied to the bucket's handle.

As the boat slow trolls either dead or live baits, the bucket is eased over the side. When the boat moves forward, the churning of the wake draws the thawing ground chum from the bucket. This technique saturates the area being trolled with the scent of food, often bringing sharks from the depths to investigate.

The effectiveness of this technique is clearly demonstrated on a flat calm day, where the slick being spread behind the boat is evidence. The key is beginning with rock-hard frozen chum, so it gradually thaws, dispensing just a nominal amount of chum. Many trollers who employ this method fish a very tight area, usually around wrecks or structure known to hold sharks.

They'll troll back and forth, often using loran or GPS to retrace their steps. Some have told me that the tiny pieces of chum will attract other species to the surface, such as mackerel, bonito, tuna, jacks, dolphin, and other pelagic species, all of which are favored table fare of sharks.

## WEED LINES

Not to be overlooked while trolling are weed lines and floating debris. Offshore trollers normally target this flotsam because within it there is often sanctuary for small baitfish. Dolphin, wahoo, marlin, and tuna are attracted to the flotsam because an easy meal is at hand. Sharks aren't much concerned with the small baitfish, but dearly enjoy a meal of the heavier game fish that are attracted to the area. Often they can be seen leisurely cruising on the surface around the flotsam, and will readily respond to a trolled baitfish or pitched bait.

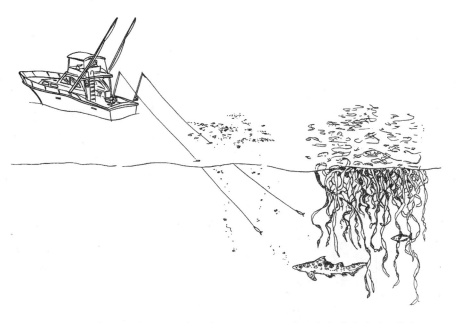

*Forage species such as anchovies and sardines congregate around the kelp beds off the California coast, on which white sea bass, sand bass, bonito, and other fish feed, and the sharks are close at hand, as a meal is readily available.*

*A variety of sharks move into the surf and coastal bays, where casters equipped with heavy surf outfits consistently score. Among the species regularly encountered are blacktip, spinner, and sandbar sharks. This beauty was hooked while the angler used a large Snap Float to carry his bait seaward with an offshore wind.*

# 9

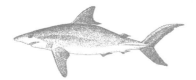

# Light Tackle

The rod was wrenched downward with a power I had yet to experience with my delicate spinning outfit. As I lifted back smartly with the rod tip, it was summarily pulled near horizontal, line screaming from the tiny Mitchell 300. For a moment I was mesmerized, standing knee-deep in the Miami Beach surf, when suddenly my adversary was airborne not more than 50 feet from where I was standing.

I can best describe the spectacular leap from the sea as resembling a 4-foot-long Polaris missile being launched, adding the unique twisting or spinning motion from which the fish derived its local name.

Just how long the fight lasted I don't know. Minutes would probably be the best assessment. It all happened so fast. The strike, line screaming from the reel, the fish in the air, leaping skyward and spinning, then crashing back in. It was repeated perhaps three or four times in all. My heart was pounding with adrenaline, and line was disappearing from the reel faster than I can describe.

Just as quickly as it began it was over. The line went limp in midair, and the blacktip shark crashed back into the sea, the Upperman Bucktail clenched in its jaw, but none the worse for its ordeal.

The year was 1953, and June and I had traveled to Miami Beach on our honeymoon. The weather in November was delight-ful; we quickly acquired suntans while at poolside and along the gorgeous beach fronting our motel. Early on we stopped at a kosher delicatessen on Collins Avenue for lunch, where the pastry chef prepared apple strudel just like my mom made. I'd often enjoy seconds.

It was then that I learned of the fine beach fishing a couple of retired regulars at the deli were enjoying. I couldn't help but over-hear the conversation at an adjoining table about jacks, ladyfish, trout, and spinners. "Spinners" were foreign to my vocabulary at the time, but I was soon to learn about an exciting game fish that fre-quented the very same waters where we swam each day.

Spinning tackle was new on the saltwater scene at the time. During my stint in the Marine Corps I'd purchased a Mitchell 300 spinning reel with a large-capacity spool and matching rod at a PX in Camp Lejeune, North Carolina. During leisure time between assignments I'd caught a lot of flounder and spotted sea trout from New River inlet. On discharge I'd also employed the fixed-spool mill back home in Jersey to catch several school stripers from the surf during their fall migration. I'd placed the spinning outfit in the trunk of the Ford as we headed south after the wedding . . . just in case.

June laughed as I repaired to poolside with spinning outfit in hand the afternoon of our luncheon encounter at the deli. The light Miami Beach surf was just too enticing.

My bride of less than a week walked with me along the beau-tiful sand as I cast a Zara Spook plug. New to spinning, after having endured the limitations of a multiplying outfit, I still marveled at the ease with which I could cast the plug on the light outfit. More surprising was the quick response my plug received from a jack crevalle, which screamed line from the reel and took what seemed like an eternity to land. It weighed perhaps 3 pounds, but fought like it weighed 10! In quick succession as we strolled the beach I landed a couple of ladyfish on a small Upperman Bucktail, and a foot-long spotted sea trout.

It was as we worked our way back to the motel that I received a strike that wrenched my rod downward with unimaginable power. So began my adventure with what is locally called a spinner shark. Incorrectly, to this day some feel the spinner shark, *Carcharhinus brevipinna* is the same as the blacktip shark, *C. limbatus.* They are different species. Whatever, the sharks with its black-tipped fins suddenly became one of my favorite light-tackle adversaries!

Since that quite accidental encounter with the spinner I've caught many species of sharks on light tackle while fishing inshore

*Captain Teddy Elrod of the* N2 Deep *prepares to release a bonnethead shark landed on light tackle while fishing off the Georgia coast. Inshore sharks include the Atlantic sharpnose, blacktip, sandbar, and spinner, which provide exciting light-tackle sport.*

waters. Most notably the blacktip, Atlantic sharpnose, dusky, lemon, sandbar, reef, and nurse sharks provide inshore anglers with many fine light-tackle opportunities. Both the smooth dogfish *Mustelus canis* and spiny dogfish *Squalus acanthias,* also provide enjoyment on light gear.

Fast-forward several years, to the day when Fred Schrier, Mark Sosin, and I, along with such notable fly casters as Joe Brooks and Hollie Hollenbeck, established what came to be known as the Salt Water Flyrodders of America in Toms River, New Jersey. At the time we fished for striped bass and bluefish in the waters of Barnegat Bay. It was while standing on a dock and receiving some casting pointers from Hollie that he invited June and me to visit with him at his home in Key Largo in the Florida Keys.

During the winter months Hollie had held forth at the then-new Ocean Reef Club in Key Largo, where he was dockmaster. With that warm invitation in hand we made the club at the tip of Key Largo our first stop the following winter.

I arrived armed with a Harnell 9-foot saltwater fly rod, a weight-forward fly line, and 200 yards of backing line loaded on a Beaudex fly reel. Hollie wasted little time in getting me aboard his flats skiff. Then it was just a five-minute ride to the pristine sand flat, where the water was barely 18 inches deep. Our target was bonefish, but a brisk wind roiled the surface and dark clouds didn't help matters, making the spotting of the bones difficult. I managed casts at a pair of bones, but had buck fever, with amateurish casts the result.

"Drop it on his nose at nine o'clock," instructed Hollie.

I spotted movement in the water, executed a false cast, and much to my surprise placed the fly just ahead of the fish. With one flash of its tail it shot forward, grabbed the Honey Blonde that Joe Brooks had given me, and screamed across the flats.

"You've got yourself a blacktip shark," said Hollie.

In the shallow water the shark literally plowed up the sand bottom and collected the golden-colored grass, carrying a load of it along the line as it turned and depleted fully half my backing. It didn't jump, but thrashed the surface to froth.

This time Lady Luck was with me, for the tiny Honey Blonde's 2/0 hook was lodged in the rubbery tissue of the blacktip's jaw. Fortunately the 12-pound tippet, while frayed, held. After a good 20 minutes Hollie reached over, grasped the exposed hook with long-nosed pliers, and freed the scrappy shark to continue its housekeeping chores on the flats.

While fishing from Virginia's beautiful barrier island beaches and the windswept sand of North Carolina's gorgeous Outer Banks, I've also experienced exciting shark fishing. On several occasions at both locations I was fishing for channel bass, the king of the mid-Atlantic surf. Using half an adult menhaden—usually the head half, as crabs were less apt to strip it from the hook—pursuing the fish often called redfish or red drum was a waiting game.

When the channel bass weren't cooperative there was the occasional southern stingray that engulfed the bait and often gave a tortuous half-hour struggle before I could slide it onto the beach, unhook it, and manhandle it back into the surf.

My first experience with sharks from the barrier islands was while fishing with Claude Rogers. It was a pleasant May morning, the sun was warm as toast, the tide had just begun to ebb, the baits were cast just beyond the breakers . . . and the channel bass wouldn't cooperate.

After a couple of hours, as I was being lulled to drowsiness by the sun, the long surf rod was practically pulled from my grasp. Reacting instinctively, I lifted back to set the hook, but the adversary responded in kind and unceremoniously began ripping line from the reel's firmly set drag.

Grinning as only the inimitable southern gentleman can, Claude beamed, "You've got yourself a granddaddy shark, Mr. Rosko!"

It took me more than an hour, after following the shark close to ½ mile down the beach, before I lifted back with rod, easing the huge shark into an incoming wave and depositing it on the beach. Claude looked at the 8/0 Octopus hook lodged in the upper jaw, grasped his pliers, and cut the leader.

*The Atlantic sharpnose shark is regularly encountered while anglers probe inshore
waters for bottom fish. For their size they provide fine sport on light spinning or
popping outfits.*

It was a sandbar shark, a 6-footer as big as I was, which we both
grabbed by the tail and dragged back into the surf, where it leisurely swam away.

Since that first sandbar shark I've landed several while fishing
the beautiful sand beaches of the mid–Atlantic. I've also caught them
while bottom fishing both from the sod banks of Jersey's Great Bay
and from a boat in Barnegat Bay. Sandbar sharks move into the shallow bay waters during May and June to provide exciting sport for
the select group of shark devotees who seek them.

On the Pacific coast the leopard shark is well within the reach
of small-boat anglers who fish the kelp beds, where light-tackle
opportunities exist to tangle with this uniquely colored shark. Many
Pacific anglers who fish from small boats always keep an outfit
rigged and ready for the leopard or other inshore sharks. Should one
show up in a chum slick, they're ready to slip on a bait and make a
presentation.

## LIGHT-TACKLE SHARKING

Within the broad spectrum of light-tackle inshore fishing for sharks are several basic outfits that will serve you well when you're fishing a locale noted for its population of toothy residents. Included would be the following:

- A light one-handed spinning rod and reel with 10- or 12-pound-test line, for casting to sharks while wading or poling the flats.

- A 10-weight fly rod and reel with 200 yards of 20-pound-test backing and Quad Tip fly line.

- An 8- or 9-foot-long surf spinning or multiplying rod and reel rated for 17- to 20-pound-test line.

- A 6-foot, 6-inch, to 7-foot medium-weight boat and multiplying casting reel rated for 20-pound-test line.

As noted earlier, many shark encounters on the fishing grounds are opportunities presented while seeking other species. Many of my first shark encounters were while aboard private charter and party boats owned by others, and often we weren't prepared. Once we commissioned the first *Linda June* I made it a practice to always have one or more of the shark outfits identified here available and ready to be instantly put into use.

Beginning with the one-handed spinning outfit, you'll note I recommend 10- or 12-pound-test line; at times I'll go to 15-pound test, though normally a lighter test. I keep this outfit rigged specifically for sharks, and the heavier line enables me to fish a tighter drag and exert more pressure once a shark is hooked.

I double the last 24 inches of my line using a surgeon's loop. I then tie a 24-inch-long piece of titanium leader wire to the loop using an Albright knot, which works ideally with titanium. To the terminal end of the leader I use an improved clinch knot to tie a 5/0 or 6/0 Claw, Beak, or Live Bait hook. If you haven't as yet used titanium leader wire, you'll find that these two knots are recom-

*Atlantic sharpnose sharks move in close to shore, where anglers enjoy fine sport with light tackle. While small, they're just as vicious as their heavyweight cousins; care must be exercised when unhooking and releasing them.*

mended by the manufacturer and ideally suited to this wire, which does not kink the way single-strand stainless-steel leader wire does.

Rigged like this the outfit is ready to slip a chunk of bonito, mullet, or sardine bait on the hook and cast to any shark patrolling the flats or skirting the edge of a kelp bed as it searches for a meal.

Some sharkers will rig the outfit with a small leadhead jig with a scented soft plastic tail, and may either fish it plain or add a small strip of bait to the hook. Both approaches receive a ready response from sharks that are hungry.

## FLY-CASTING TACKLE AND FLIES

With the fly-casting outfit I use an 8-foot tapered fluorocarbon leader, tapering from a 30-pound butt section to a 17- or 20-pound-test tippet. I follow the same procedure outlined above, with a surgeon's loop, then an Albright knot to attach 12 inches of titanium leader wire, and finally an improved clinch knot to attach the fly. The short leader adequately turns over even a large, heavy fly, and its test is sufficiently strong to enable you to bully a shark once hooked.

You'll note I recommend Scientific Anglers Quad Tip fly lines, which give you the entire range from a floating line, to intermediate sink rates, to a high-density tip that gets deep. In this way you're able to utilize a looping system to change fly-line tips. This enables you to select one tip section to suit conditions on the flats where a floating line is needed, and a different one for probing the depths if you observe sharks cruising above a reef where a high-density line will get your fly deep.

There's a wide selection of flies that will tempt strikes from sharks. *Keep it simple* is perhaps the best advice I can offer, for sharks are most often cruising along, looking for something to eat. When it comes to shark fishing, the exotically tied flies are more for the fly fisherman than the shark. Basic patterns, such as the Clouser when you want the fly taken deep with a high-density line, or a Lefty's Deceiver when probing the shallow water of the flats with a floating fly, will well serve your needs. The Half & Half—actually a combination of the Clouser and Deceiver—is also a good choice, as is the Bighorn Sardine. Big flies like the Enrico's Mullet or Mackerel

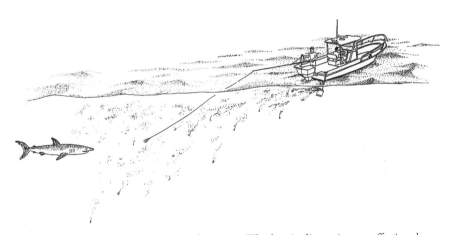

*Fly casting to sharks requires unlimited patience. The key is dispensing an effective chum line to attract the sharks to the surface. A large bunker fly, dipped in chum to give it scent, often proves very effective. Most fly casters use a short titanium wire leader, which is the only leader wire that can be tied using a conventional improved clinch knot.*

are also good choices. Lean toward larger flies, rather than smaller, with 3/0 hooks a good choice, as the majority of sharks you're apt to encounter will range from 5 to 50 pounds.

Even if you're fortunate enough to hook one that reaches the century mark, you should be able to handle it with a 10-weight outfit rigged as just described. Boat handling will be important too, as you may well land the blacktip or sand shark ½ mile or more from where you hooked it. During the initial phase of the battle, even heavy pressure on your part won't do much to slow down a feisty shark.

While fly-fishing purists may shudder at the suggestion of dipping a fly in bunker oil, saturating it with ground chum, this approach gives a touch of scent to the fly, an important consideration when tempting sharks to strike. The nominal scent, coupled with a presentation that places the fly within a few feet of its cruise path, will usually entice a strike.

## SURF FISHING FOR SHARKS

Early encounters while catching sharks from the barrier island and Outer Banks surf were often a matter of luck: The hook penetrated the jaw and the shark wasn't able to bite through a monofilament leader intended for channel bass. You'll learn quickly that Lady Luck is not always with you, and if you want to regularly land sharks hooked in the surf you had better go equipped with a wire leader.

*Keep it simple* applies equally to a surf rig for sharks. I prefer to double the last 3 feet of the terminal end of my line using a surgeon's loop; this is the section of line that gets a lot of pressure and potential abrasion while casting, and also while resting on the bottom. It also provides a good handhold to drag a shark from the surf.

I then use a uniknot to attach the double line to a medium-sized three-way swivel. For many years I used No. 8 or 9 stainless-steel leader wire to fashion a 3-foot-long leader. A haywire twist is then used to attach the leader to the swivel and hook. You might want to consider using titanium wire in lieu of the stainless steel, as it does not have memory, and as such does not kink and break

*Large coastal sharks test surf anglers and their tackle to the limit. Bottom fishing with a chunk of menhaden or a whole spot is the way to coax strikes from these formidable fighters, which require heavy surf tackle in order to land. This big shark was hauled back into the surf and promptly released.*

should a shark get twisted up in it. Use an ordinary improved clinch knot to secure the titanium wire to the swivel and hook.

A size 7/0 or 8/0 Claw, Beak, or Octopus hook is a good choice when seeking sharks from shore, as you'll be using big baits.

To complete the rig, tie a 6- to 8-inch-long piece of monofilament line with a loop in the end of it to the remaining eye of the three-way swivel. Your best choice of sinker style for the surf is a pyramid, as this holds best in a rough surf. The sinker is easily slipped onto the looped monofilament tied to the three-way swivel. The size of the sinker you use will be determined by the surf condition, with 3 or 4 ounces adequate in a calm surf and 6 ounces often necessary when conditions are rough.

You can use almost any small fish as bait when seeking sharks from the surf or adjoining bay beaches. Among the most popular baits are menhaden and mullet, although spot, croaker, mackerel, or herring may be used. I prefer the head section of the fish as the bait of choice, as it's tough and bony, and crabs have more difficulty stripping it from the hook than they do with the softer tail section. Make a cut at a 45-degree angle from just behind the head, downward toward the stomach. It's fine if the entrails hang freely, as they emit the shark-attracting scent that's so important.

Insert the hook into the lower jaw and out the upper. A mossbunker or mullet head bait hooked in this manner is difficult for other small fish in the area to rip from the hook, and when a shark happens by it will inhale it in an instant.

Along much of the middle and south Atlantic coast, and along portions of the Gulf coast frequented by inshore sharks and dogfish,

*The spiny dogfish is found along the Atlantic coast and often considered a pest by many anglers. This was one of several caught by Jennifer Basilio, the author's granddaughter who prepared the shark illustrations in this book, during an otherwise uneventful day of surf fishing. Many people dice the dogfish meat into small pieces and use it to prepare fish-and-chips, a popular dish among seafood lovers.*

there are often sandbars paralleling the beach for miles. At irregular intervals there are breaks in the bars, often called holes, where the water is deeper than the adjoining bars. The sharks use these breaks to move inside the bars on a flooding tide. There they cruise up and down the sluices where the water ranges from 3 to 6 feet deep, and where the forage is plentiful.

Your best choice of location is to fish your bait in the deep holes between the bars. This is the area transited by the sharks as they move inshore on the flooding tide, and then exit on the ebb.

You can also score by fishing in the sluices inside the bars. I caution you to not try to cast beyond the bars; it's almost impossible to do and serves no purpose as the sharks and other game fish are most often feeding right in the wash inside the bar formations.

From the Carolinas to Florida there are many anglers who fish for sharks from coastal piers and the surf while using a float rig. From a pier you can simply drift out the float, but shore-based anglers require an offshore wind so that they can ease their float rig into the water and then let the wind carry it seaward to the sharks that regularly cruise along the shoreline.

The most popular method of rigging is to use a Snap Float, which can be positioned at a desired location on the line to suspend your bait at a specific depth. When a shark is hooked the Snap Float literally snaps closed, and slides on the line as the shark is fought.

The terminal rigging for shark fishing while using a float while fishing from the surf or piers usually consists of 6 to 8 feet of No. 10 or 12 stainless-steel leader wire, a 150-pound-test Spro power swivel, and an 8/0 or 9/0 hook.

A live bait such as a croaker, spot, grunt, or pinfish is best. In addition to its scent it will emit distress signals, both of which readily attract hungry sharks.

## SHARKING IN BAY WATERS

Sandbar sharks in particular often take up residence in bay waters, where anglers regularly score while casting from the marsh banks.

Boat fishermen target the same blacktip, bull, dusky, and sand-bar sharks often caught from surf and bay waters. A favorite technique is to anchor in a thoroughfare frequented by the sharks as they move from deep water on a flooding tide. For it's on the flood that they move onto the shallow flats of the Florida Keys and along the Gulf coast, or work along the channel edges searching for a meal.

Use the same terminal rigging and baiting technique described for surf fishing. While anchoring is the preferred method, I've fished with some Florida Keys guides who would drift the thoroughfares, especially on windy, cloudy days where the overcast made flats fishing virtually impossible. We often scored with sharks of respectable size, including 5- and 6-footers, that many people don't even realize are regularly frequenting these waterways.

I've also used this same boat rod and terminal rigging while anchored on inshore reefs of the Keys and fishing for yellowtail snappers and groupers. We usually fish for the smaller species with a light spinning or popping outfit, but always have a heavier boat rod rigged for shark. The arrival of a hungry shark is often disclosed when you suddenly hook up with one of the marauders as you're reeling in a yellowtail or grouper . . . and instead wind up with half a fish, or no fish at all.

That's the time we'll break out the 20-pound boat rod, bait up with a live pinfish or grunt hooked through the lips, and cast it out. The distress signals transmitted by the hooked baitfish quickly arouse the interest of any shark roaming the reef, and it'll engulf it quickly.

On several occasions I've witnessed the same shark being caught twice within a few hours' time while fishing the reefs. The shark is brought alongside and the leader cut, whereupon it goes right back to biting off yellowtail snappers and groupers. Finally a hook bait is put over, whereupon it quickly gobbles up another grunt or pinfish!

During recent years the media has had a field day with shark sightings in shallow water, especially in Florida and along the Gulf coast. There have been many serious encounters with swimmers and even careless boaters who dangle legs in the warm water. Boaters

*While bonefish and permit are the favored target of fishermen in the Florida Keys, it's often a prowling spinner shark that saves an otherwise uneventful day. Several species of sharks roam the flats and present a target, as pictured here, ready to take a small bait, jig, or fly.*

and swimmers should always use caution when frequenting waters where sharks may be in residence.

In my view these sharks have been there for years, actively feeding on the plentiful forage found in the inshore waters. I caution fishermen to avoid chumming or fishing in areas shared with swimmers. There are plenty of other waters where you can target your favorite sharks without chum exciting their interest in the presence of bathers.

The inshore sharks you're apt to catch on the flats, along inshore thoroughfares, and from the surf quite honestly don't compare to the mako, thresher, and porbeagle found in offshore waters. Yet when sought with tackle suited to their size they provide an exciting challenge to the light-tackle angler. Because they play such an important role in maintaining the delicate balance of nature in the marine environment, always take care to release them promptly.

*Captain Teddy Elrod prepares to release a small blacktip shark. Notice the pronounced black tips at the end of the shark's pectoral fins and on the dorsal fin.*

# 10

# A Valuable Resource

The National Marine Fisheries Service establishes rules and regulations that govern landings of sharks from coastal waters of the United States. It has the responsibility of establishing quotas for commercial landings of sharks and bag limits for sportfishermen. Its objective is to maintain sustainable fisheries for the many species of sharks found in our coastal waters.

The group has established three categories for sharks that are all-encompassing, and while many of the sharks are not the targets of anglers, I'm including the breakdown of all the sharks in each category to provide an understanding of the magnitude of the shark fishery as it applies to both commercial fishermen and recreational anglers.

*Pelagic sharks* include the bigeye sixgill, bigeye thresher, blue, longfin mako, oceanic whitetip, porbeagle, sevengill, shortfin mako, sixgill, and thresher.

The *large coastal shark* category includes basking, bignose, black-tip, bull, Caribbean reef, dusky, Galapagos, great hammerhead, lemon, narrowtooth, night, nurse, sandbar, sand tiger, scalloped hammerhead, silky, smooth hammerhead, spinner, tiger, whale, and white.

The *small coastal sharks* include the Atlantic angel, Atlantic sharpnose, blacknose, bonnethead, Caribbean sharpnose, finetooth, and smalltail.

Because National Marine Fisheries Service regulations concerning shark species and bag limits are susceptible to change, it's important that you monitor them to prevent inadvertent violation.

The Apex Predators Program is located at the Narragansett, Rhode Island, laboratory of the National Marine Fisheries Service, Northeast Fisheries Science Center. This is one of three programs in the Population Biology Branch of the Fisheries and Ecosystems Monitoring and Analysis Division. Its mission is to conduct life history studies of commercially and recreationally important shark species; research is focused on migrations, age and growth, reproductive biology, and feeding ecology. Information gathered from these research programs provides baseline biological data for the management of large sharks.

You can access the Apex Predators Web site at *http://na.nefsc. noaa.gov/sharks/* and be immediately updated with the current regulations and a wealth of information on sharks of interest to recreational anglers.

Toward this end I've stopped killing even mako sharks, although I must admit that I certainly used to enjoy them on the dinner table. Indeed, in many of my prior books I asked my wife, June, to prepare a chapter including her favorite fish recipes. I declined to do so in this book as I felt it might encourage anglers to kill more sharks because of their fine table quality.

The dilemma that results when it comes to killing sharks for the table is that if you kill the small mako and other edible sharks, they will not have had an opportunity to reproduce or pup. On the other end of the spectrum, it seems wrong to kill a huge mako that has just reached an age when it can reproduce. In my view the best alternative is to just not kill sharks for the table, thus contributing in some small way to the rebuilding of the shark populations off our coasts.

The last 20 years have seen a drastic decline in most shark populations. This decline came about as a result of increased fishing pressure by both commercial and recreational anglers. In the years of plenty there was never a thought given to the fact that the populations could be severely depleted by overfishing. As in so many other fisheries, by the time it was realized that shark populations were reaching levels

*Pete Casale prepares to release a blue shark brought to boatside by the author. Unless a shark is to be used for the table, it should be promptly released so that future generations will have the opportunity to pursue these fine game fish.*

that could jeopardize their survival they were at a point where there was no easy remedy. In my view, even with sound regulations, it may take another 20 years for the populations to rebound to a level where taking sharks for the table would be appropriate.

I just enjoy catching and releasing sharks. From all I have been able to learn, and have observed over the years, the survival rate of sharks released at boatside is extraordinarily high. In fact, survival is much higher than among most fish caught and released by recreational anglers.

One option available to sportfishermen is that of tagging sharks prior to release. My good friend Jack Casey, who spent his career at the National Marine Fisheries Service laboratories at Sandy Hook, New Jersey and Narragansett, Rhode Island, advocated tagging, as it added a new dimension to shark fishing and provided scientific data via tag returns, resulting in a win–win situation.

Jack's retired, but Nancy Kohler continues in his stead as the shark program coordinator. She welcomes angler participation in the NMFS Cooperative Shark Tagging Program. As I was preparing this book we spoke concerning the great opportunity that anglers have to tag and release sharks.

Nancy was kind enough to provide much of the research and tag return information included herein that I found particularly informative and interesting.

The Cooperative Shark Tagging Program was initiated in 1962 with an initial group of less than 100 volunteers under Jack Casey's leadership. The program has expanded in subsequent years and currently includes thousands of volunteers from along the Atlantic and Gulf coasts and Europe.

The tagging methods used have been virtually unchanged during the past four decades. The two principal tags that are in use are a fin tag or rototag, and a dart tag or M tag. The rototag is a two-piece, plastic cattle-ear-type tag that is inserted through the first dorsal fin. As the tagging program expanded to include thousands of volunteer fishermen, the dart tag was developed to be easily and safely applied to sharks in the water. The M tag is composed of a stainless-steel dart head, monofilament line, and a Plexiglas capsule containing a vinyl plastic legend with return instructions printed in English, Spanish, French, Japanese, and Norwegian. These dart tags, in use since 1965, are implanted in the back musculature near the base of the first dorsal fin. More recently, a Hallprint tag has been used on a limited basis for small sharks in the nursery areas.

Numbered tags are sent to volunteer participants on self-addressed return postcards for recording tagging information (date, location, gear, size and sex of shark), along with a tagging needle, tagging instructions, an *Anglers Guide to Sharks of the Northeastern United States,* and a current *Shark Tagger* newsletter. The newsletter is an annual summary of the previous year's tag and recapture data and biological studies on sharks; it's sent to all participants in the tagging program. Tagging studies have been mostly single-release events in which recreational and commercial fishermen make recoveries. When a previously tagged shark is recaught, information similar to that obtained at tagging is requested from the recapturer. Since 1988, a hat with an embroidered logo has been sent to anglers providing tag return information.

Since the tagging program began more than 175,000 sharks have been tagged and released, and more than 10,000 have been recaptured. This includes 40 species, with recaptures of 32 species. Eighty-six percent of the recaptures are made up of seven species: blue shark, sandbar shark, tiger shark, shortfin mako, lemon shark, dusky shark, and nurse shark. The rate of recapture ranges from 1.4 percent for the Atlantic sharpnose shark to 10.6 percent for the nurse shark.

Recreational anglers using rod and reel accomplished the majority of the tagging for all species combined. Distances traveled among the 32 species ranged from no movement to 3,740 nautical miles. In total, one species (the blue shark) traveled distances of more than 3,000 nautical miles; three species traveled between 2,000 and 3,000 nautical miles (the shortfin mako, dusky, and sandbar sharks); and eight species (the tiger, bignose, Galapagos, bigeye thresher, night, oceanic whitetip, blacktip, and porbeagle) voyaged 1,000 to 2,000 nautical miles. Seven species traveled distances between 500 and 1,000 nautical miles: the scalloped hammerhead, spinner, longfin mako, silky, sand tiger, Atlantic sharpnose, and white shark.

The longest time at liberty for any shark in the tagging program is 27.8 years. Overall, 1 species (the sandbar shark) has been at liberty more than 20 years; 3 species have been at liberty between 10 and 20 years (the dusky, night, and tiger sharks); and 13 have been at liberty between 5 and 10 years: the scalloped hammerhead, shortfin mako, blacknose, bignose, porbeagle, blue, thresher, nurse, Atlantic sharpnose, blacktip, silky, bull, and bigeye thresher sharks.

These results certainly confirm the great value tagging has in both preserving and conserving shark stocks, particularly by recreational anglers. Data from tagging programs provide valuable information on migration. The need for international cooperation is underscored by the fact that many shark species have wide-ranging distributions, frequently traverse national boundaries, and are exploited by multinational fisheries.

The tagging program is also an important means to increase biological understanding of sharks and to obtain information for rational resource management. The tagging of sharks provides information on stock identity, movements and migration, abundance, age and growth, mortality, and behavior.

This is especially true where shark fishing tournaments are held with special divisions for tagging and releasing, rather than bringing sharks to the dock. Toward this end I encourage all tournaments to establish a tag-and-release division, using tags provided by NMFS.

Tags and tagging instructions, plus a copy of Jack Casey's fine booklet on shark identification, are available free of charge. To obtain the packet you need only write a short letter of intent to participate in the Cooperative Shark Tagging Program. Mail it directly to Cooperative Shark Tagging Program, National Marine Fisheries Service, 28 Tarzwell Drive, Narragansett, RI 02882. They will get your packet out promptly and will also replenish your tags as you place them in the toothy adversaries.

From my observations Pacific coast shark anglers have also been far responsive to the tag-and-release concept than Atlantic or Gulf coast anglers. Keith Poe is without question one of the West's dominant shark taggers. He has consistently placed among the top individual anglers who tag and release sharks, having recognized at an early age the importance of understanding more about sharks, shortfin makos in particular, and especially providing them the opportunity to breed.

Keith participates in the California Department of Fish and Game's volunteer pelagic shark tagging program, which began back in 1983. I first learned of this effort when I read Keith's extremely informative article in *Big Game Fishing Journal* magazine in 1998. This program has resulted in thousands of shortfin mako sharks being tagged since its inception. Remarkably, this tremendous tagging effort has been accomplished by a small group of dedicated taggers!

Keith's personal log discloses that he's tagged a remarkable number of shortfin makos and other sharks of various species. He's found that the tagging is as much fun as the catching, and certainly more responsible than indiscriminate killing of this important resource.

Pacific coast anglers interested in participating in the California Division of Fish and Game's excellent volunteer shark tagging program can obtain a tagging kit and supply of tags by corresponding with John Ugoretz, Marine Biologist, California Department of Fish & Game, Shark Tagging Program, 300 Golden Shore, Suite 50, Long Beach, California 90802.

*Many shark fishermen have made a practice of keeping but a single edible shark for the table each season. Promptly cleaned, and properly cared for, many sharks are fine table fare. Ken Beyer steaks a big mako, which was promptly iced to ensure its arrival home in mint condition.*

Sharks are too valuable a resource to succumb to irresponsible individuals and organizations that promote tournaments that kill countless numbers just to prove that the anglers know how to catch a shark.

Tournament promoters invariably have an agenda, and from what I've observed it's most often to make money. Hundreds of boats sailing from a tournament marina generates revenue via fuel and bait sales, lodging, meals, tackle sales, and myriad other sources. Plus, of course, the registration fees, of which the promoters of some tournaments retain a portion.

If perchance tournament fishing fascinates you, then by all means consider participating when tagging and releasing sharks is encouraged or where minimum sizes are enforced. I have no quarrel with a rally of anglers that includes divisions for this important pursuit that lets you enjoy every aspect of shark fishing on a contemplative level, yet removes the competitive fervor of just killing sharks for no legitimate reason. Killing juvenile sharks that haven't had an opportunity to reproduce especially appalls me.

Tagging adds an entirely new dimension to shark fishing, for you're not only directly contributing to the preservation of sharks but also helping expand scientific data as to growth rates, travel, and seasonal migrations. It's not at all unusual for many pelagic sharks to travel thousands of miles as they roam the waters of the world.

Adding to the personal excitement of the tagging experience is when you receive notification that one of the sharks that you tagged has been captured, its tag removed, tagged again, and set free!

# CONCLUSION

As I complete this book I hope it becomes the beginning of a great opportunity to expand your angling to include shark fishing. You'll find shark species in almost all of the waters you plan to fish. In many cases, much as I've done over the years, you'll develop an attachment, whether it be to a sickle-tailed thresher shark off San Diego, a sleek blacktip on a Keys tidal flat, or a high-jumping mako in the northeast canyons.

Shark fishing is addictive. Being successful at it is not happenstance. It takes study, application, perseverance, and your tackle and equipment working in concert to hook and bring a shark within range of the tagging stick, and then release it. Only when you've experienced the adrenaline rush of going toe-to-toe with a big shark will you join that growing fraternity who love shark fishing. I just love every minute I spend seeking these tough adversaries. Join me and you'll open a whole new angling horizon that you'll enjoy for a lifetime.

# INDEX